This Book belongs to

....

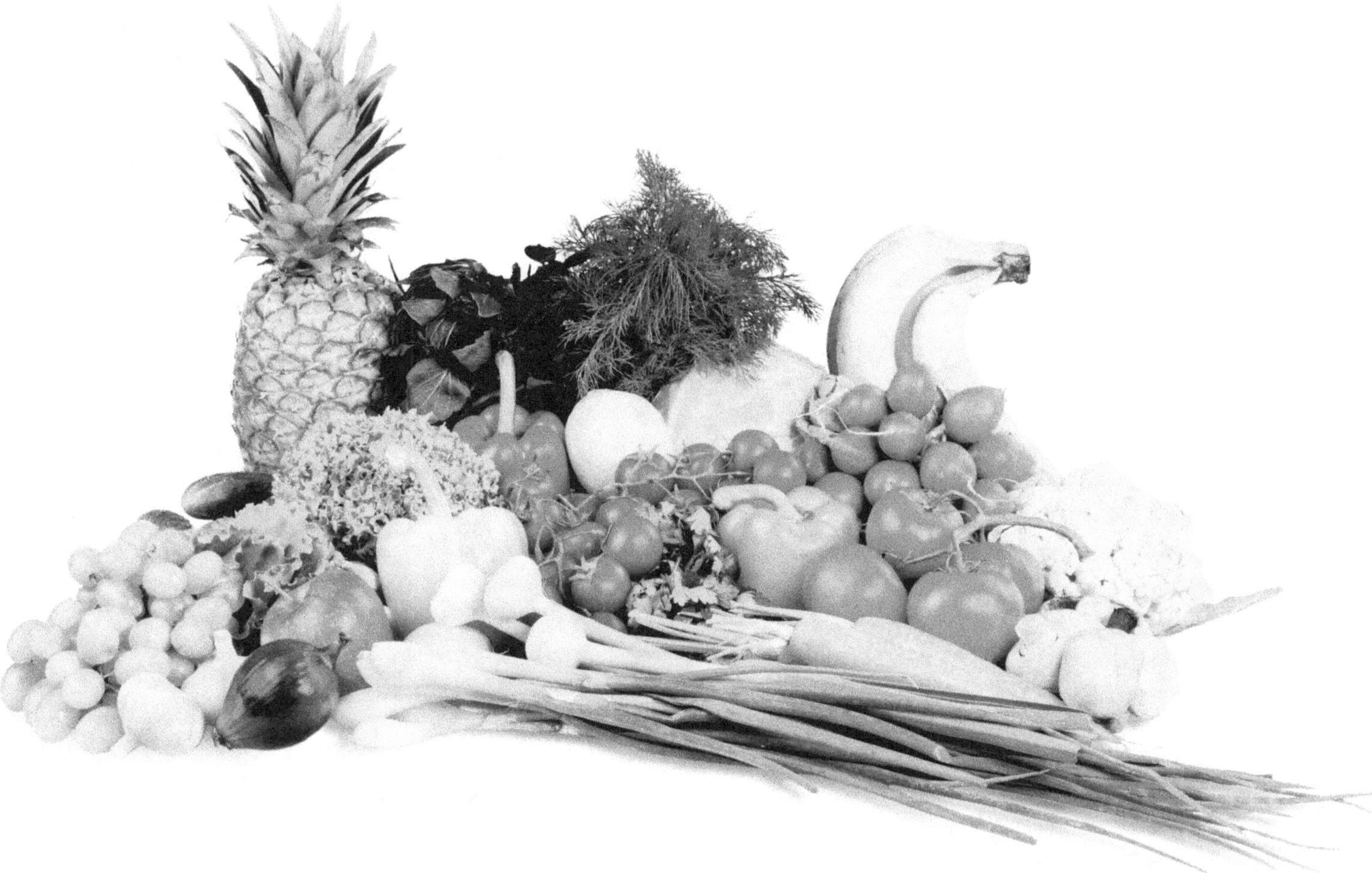

A for

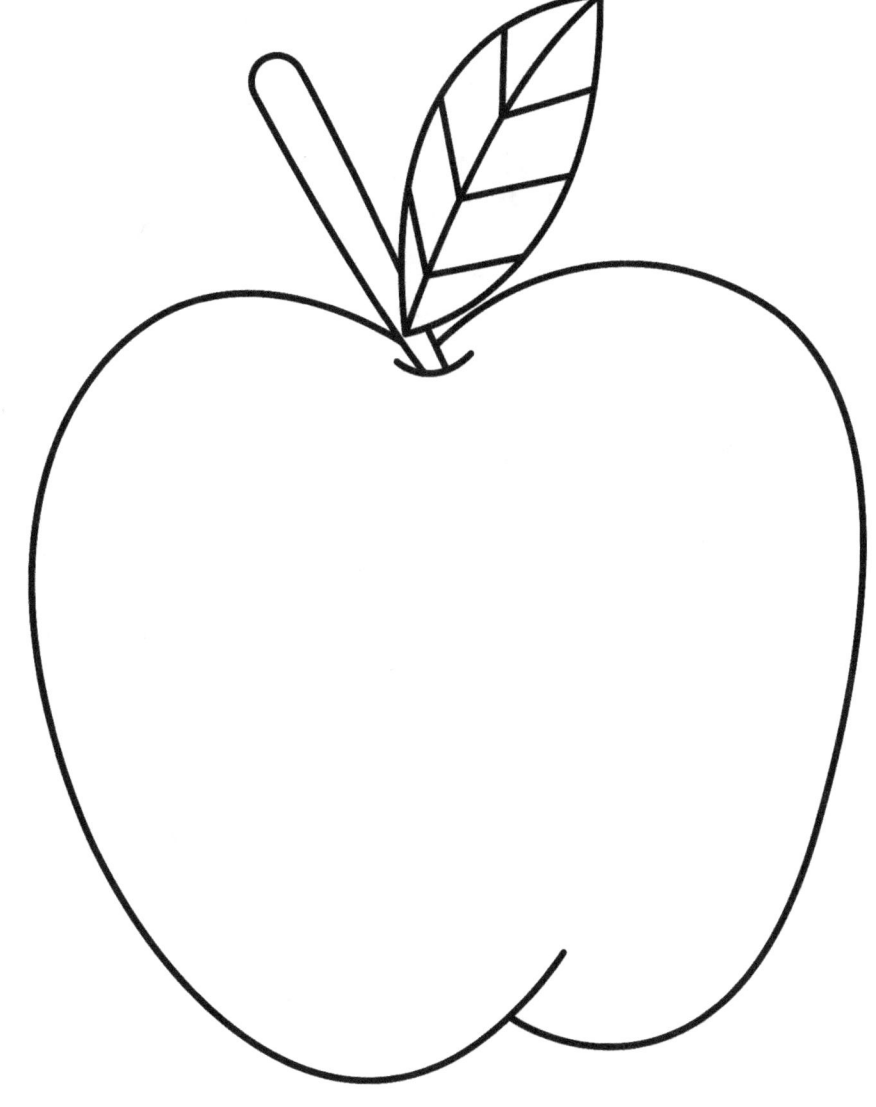

Apple

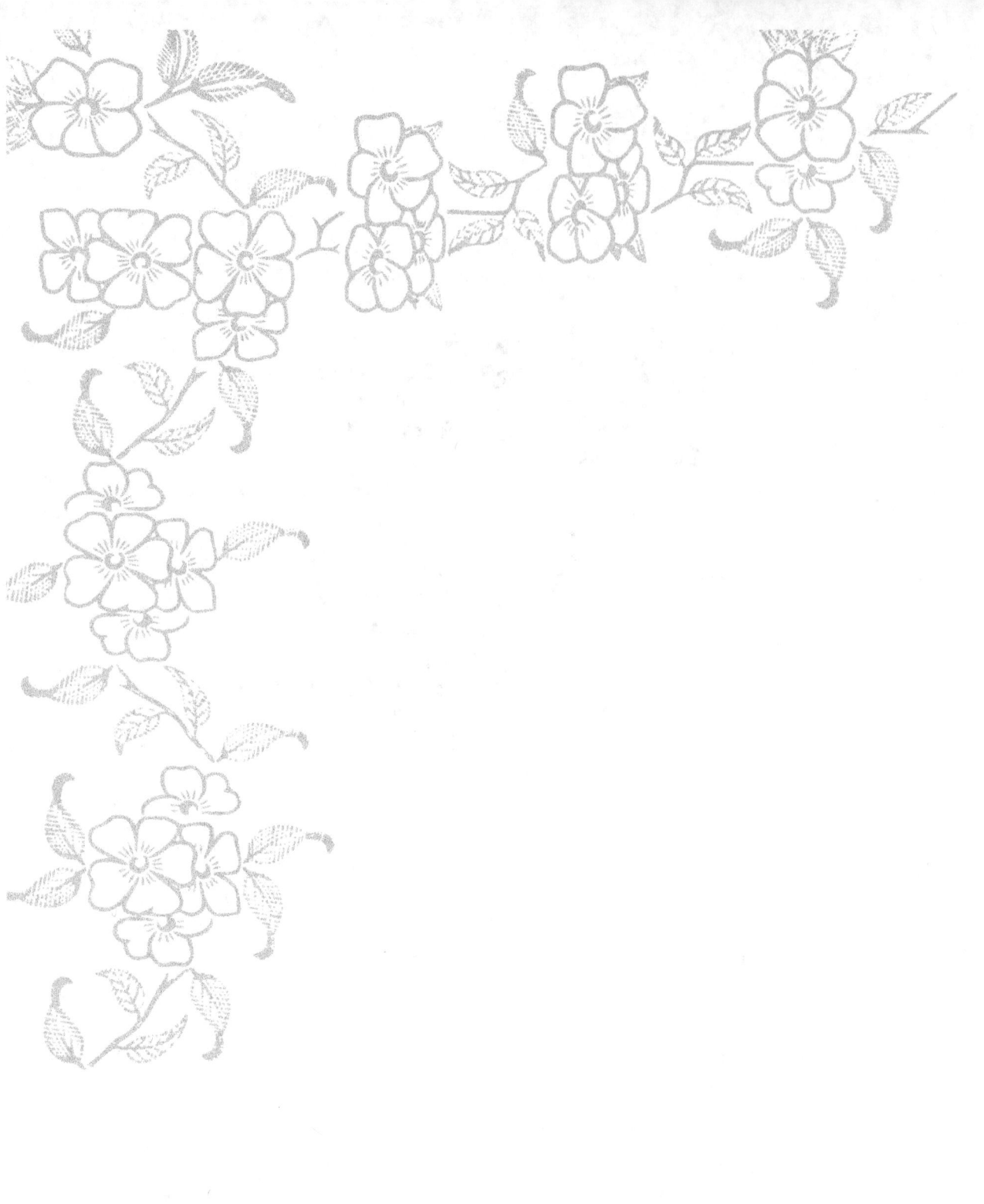

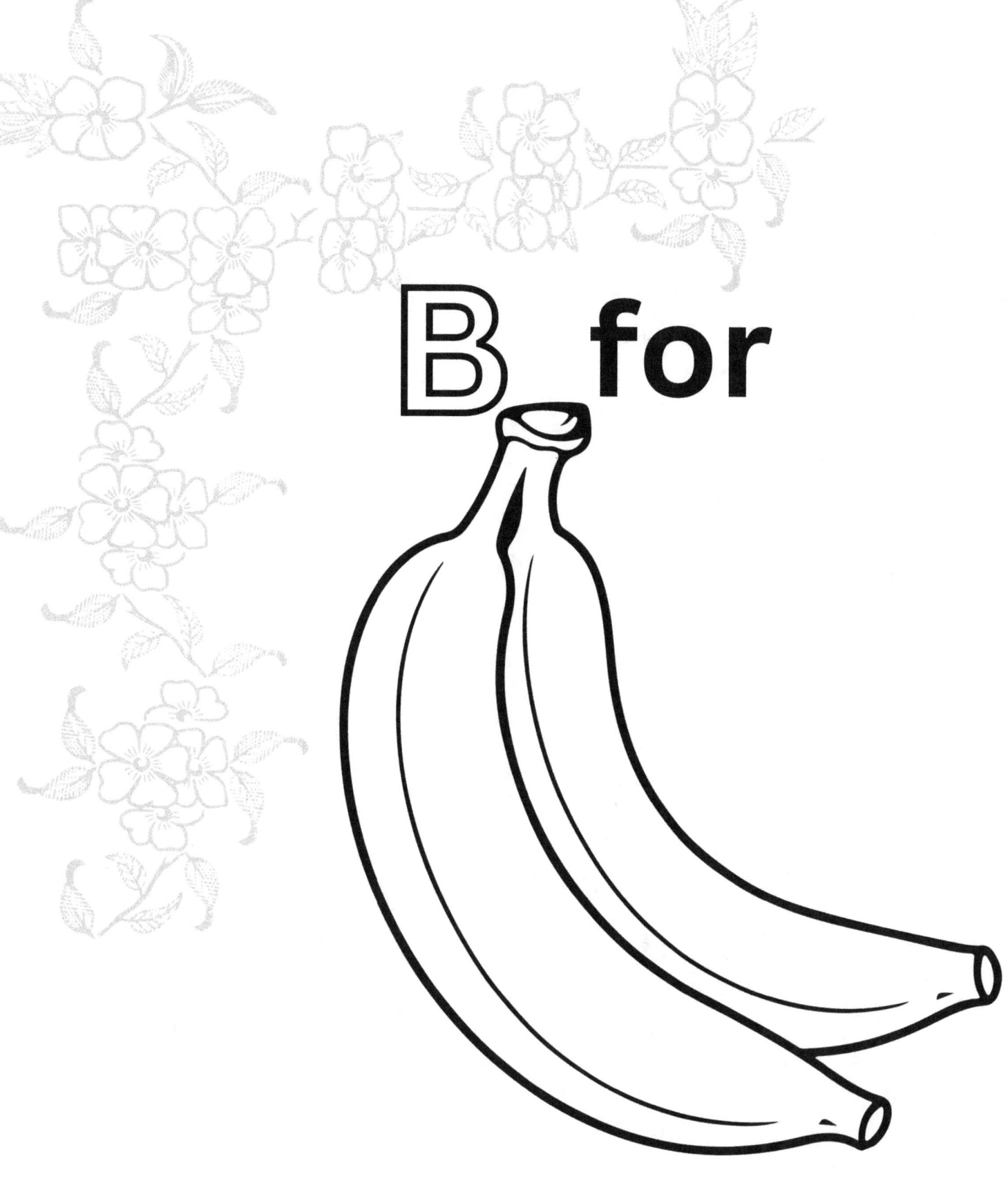

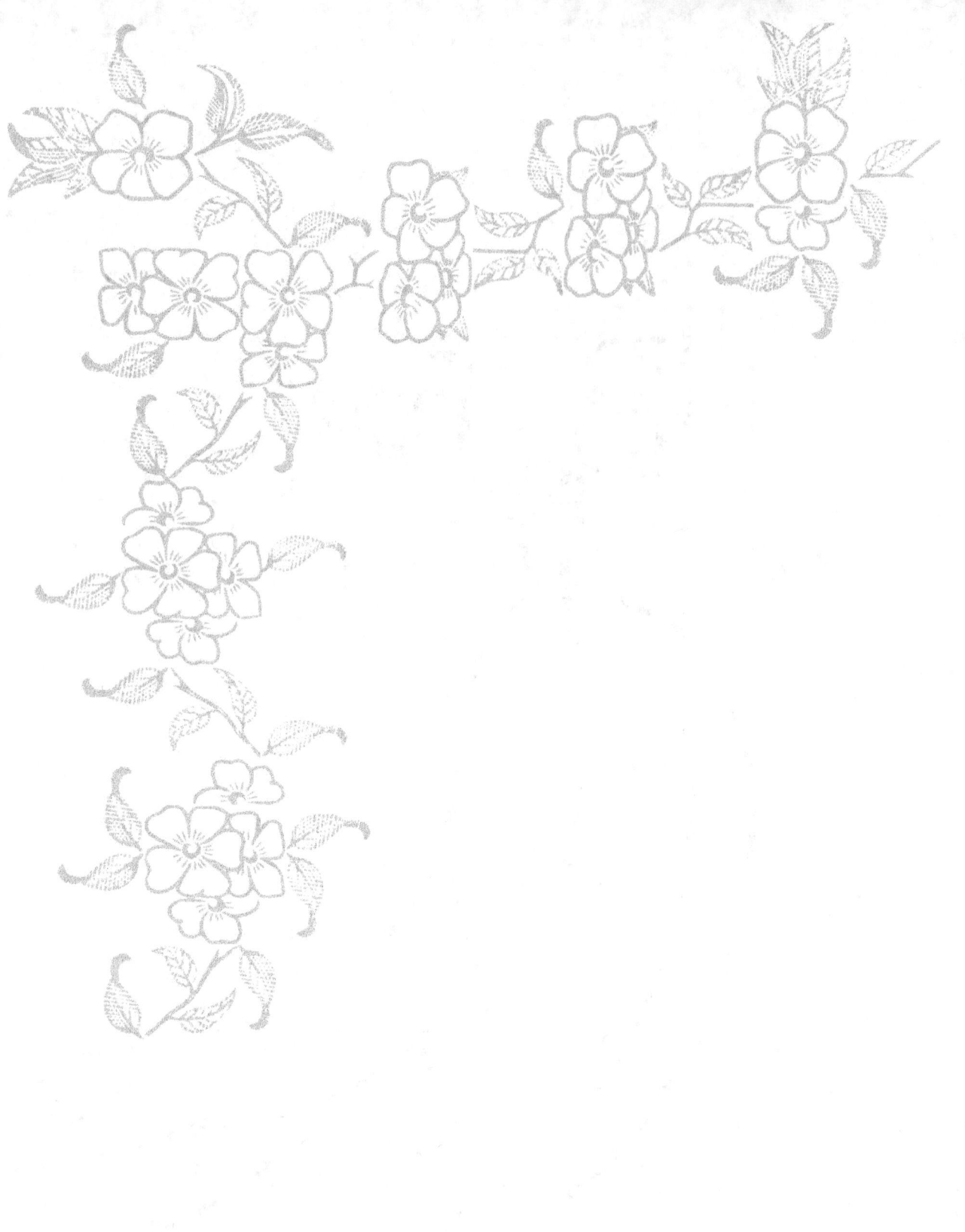

C for

Cherry

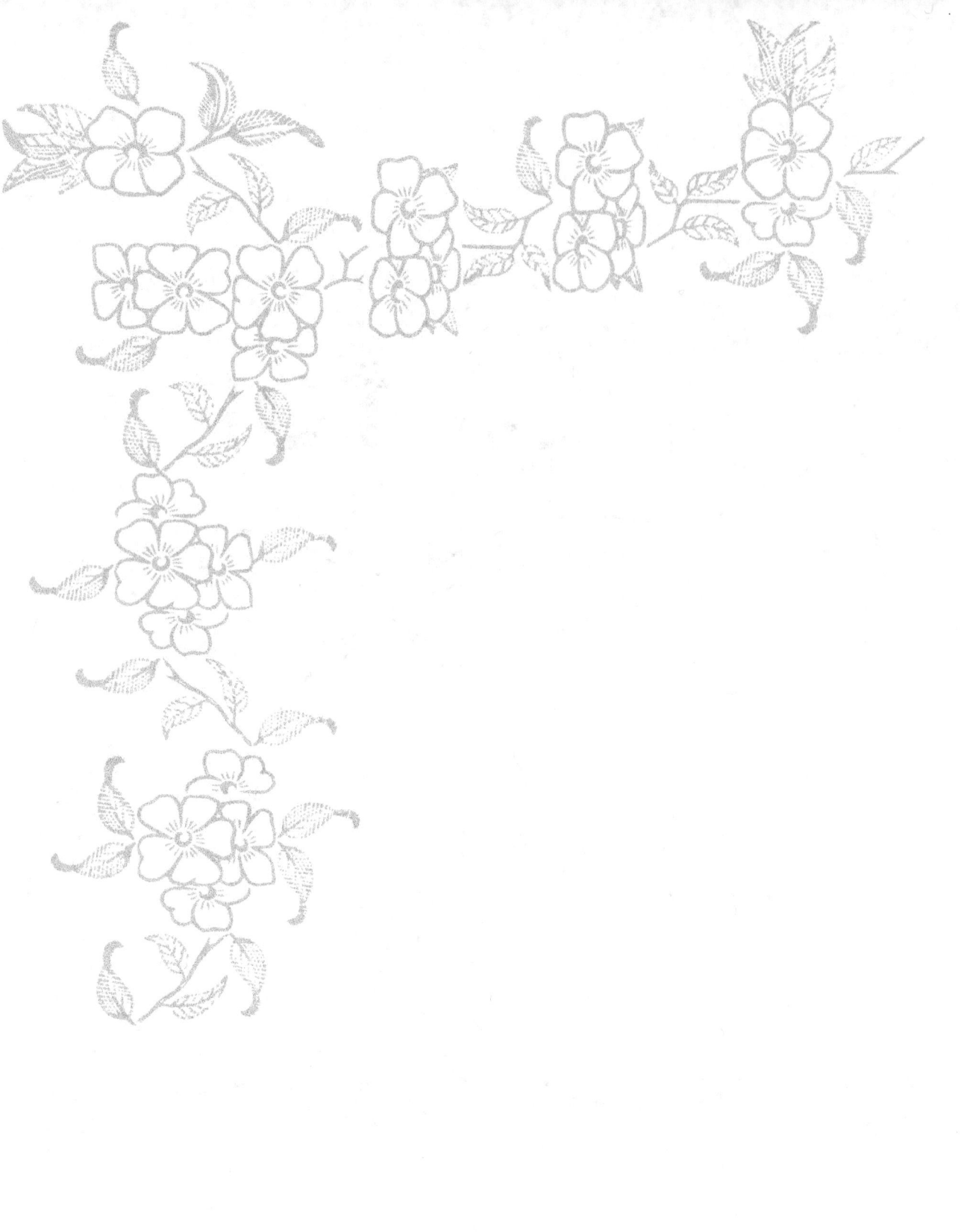

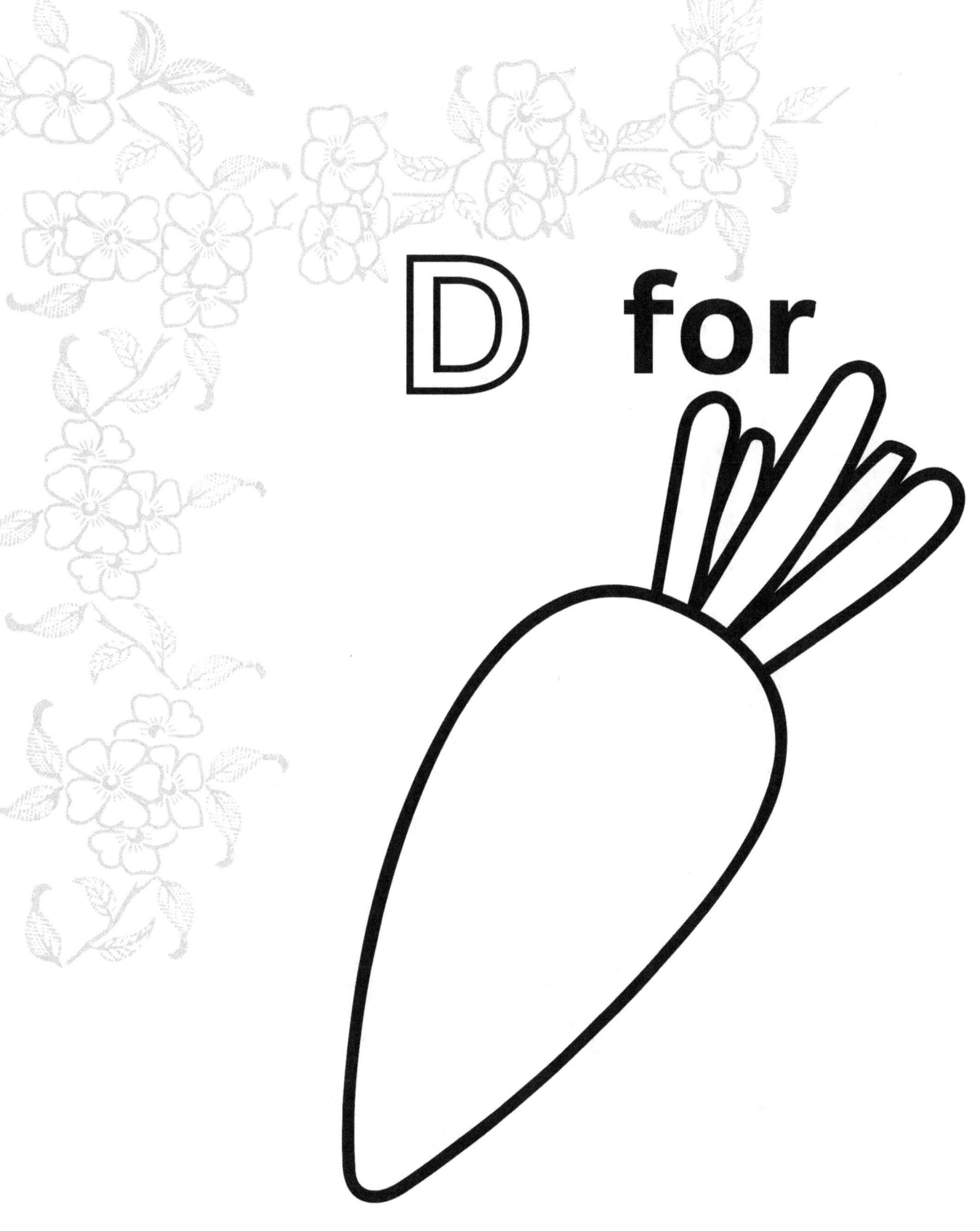

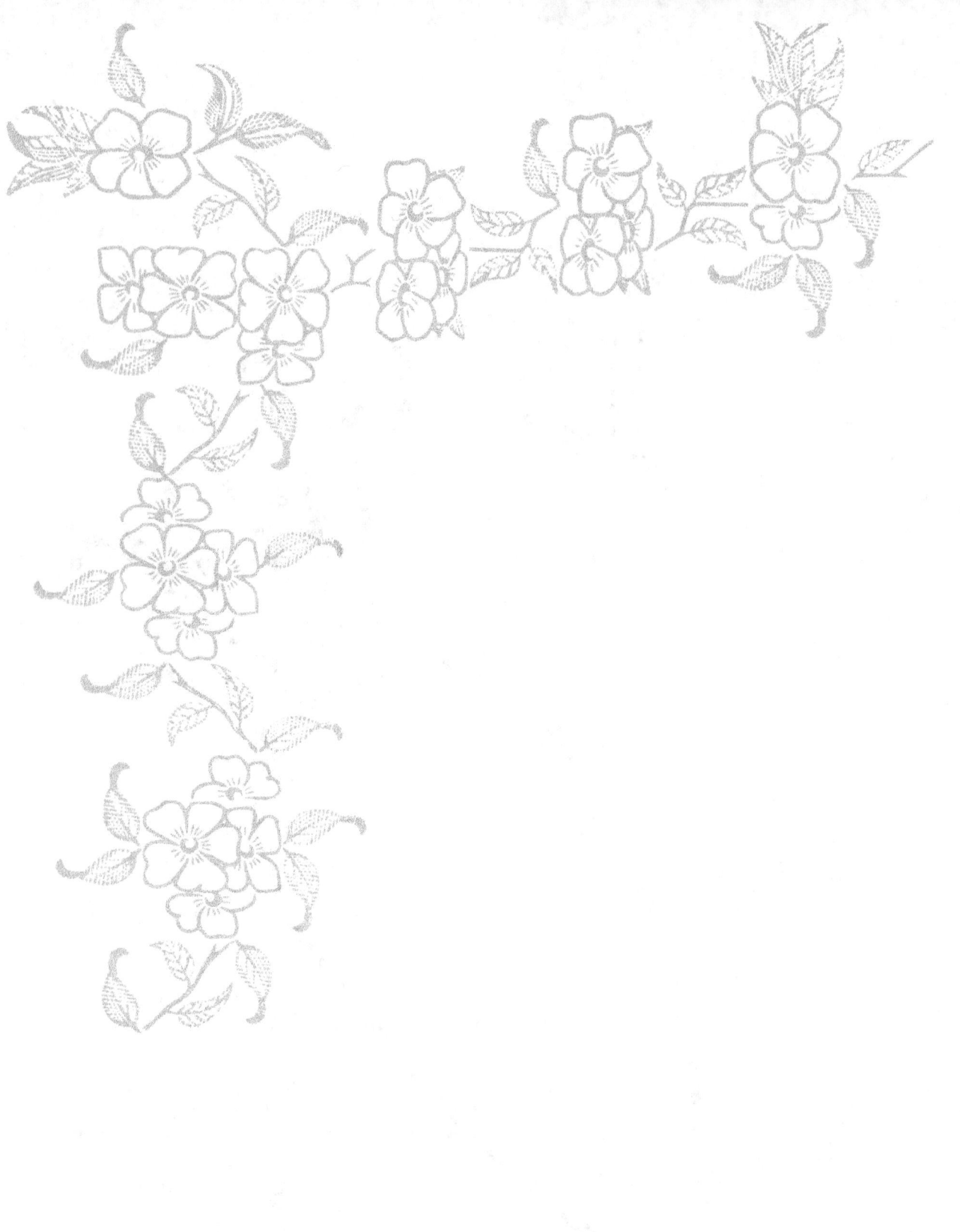

E for

Elderberry

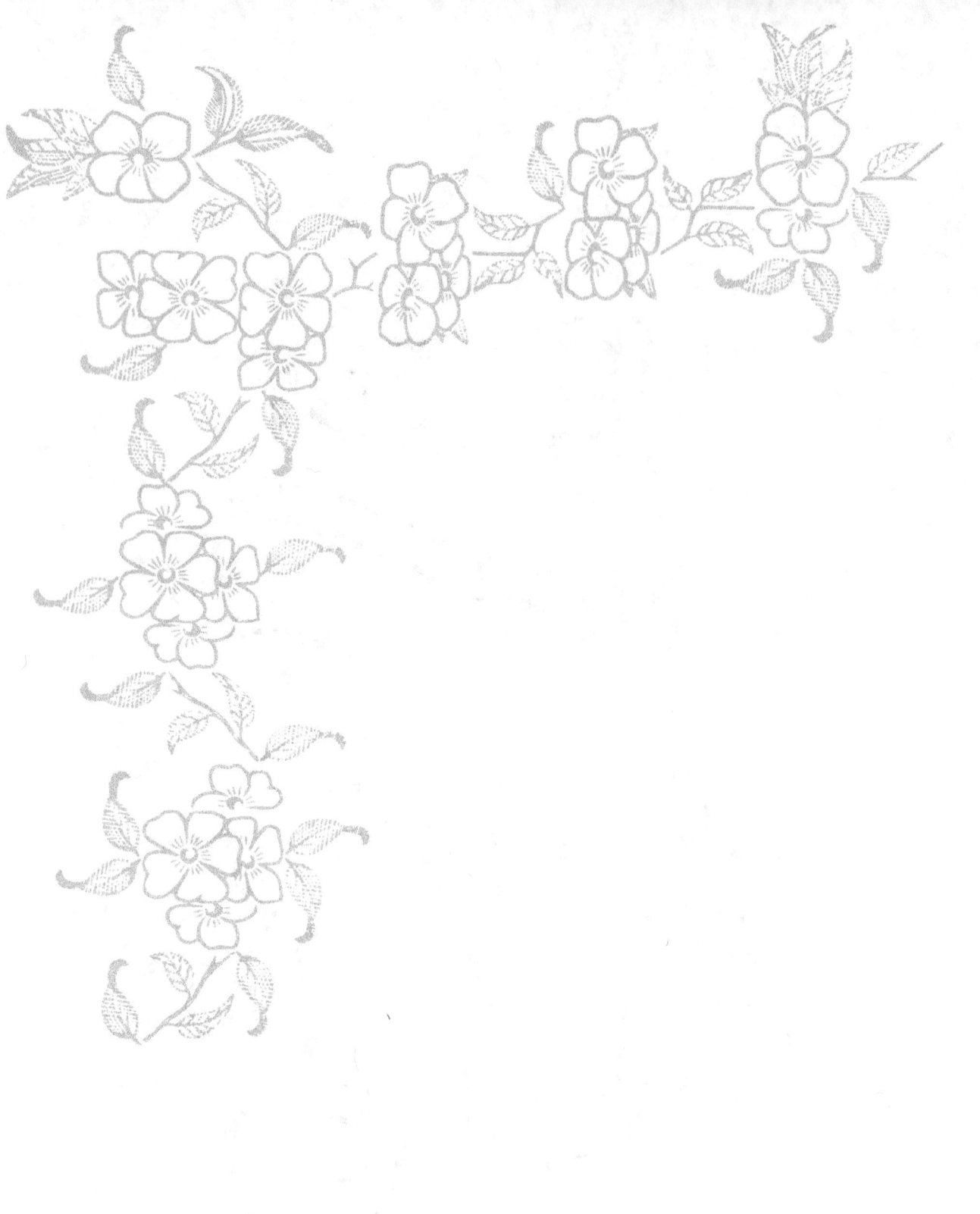

F for

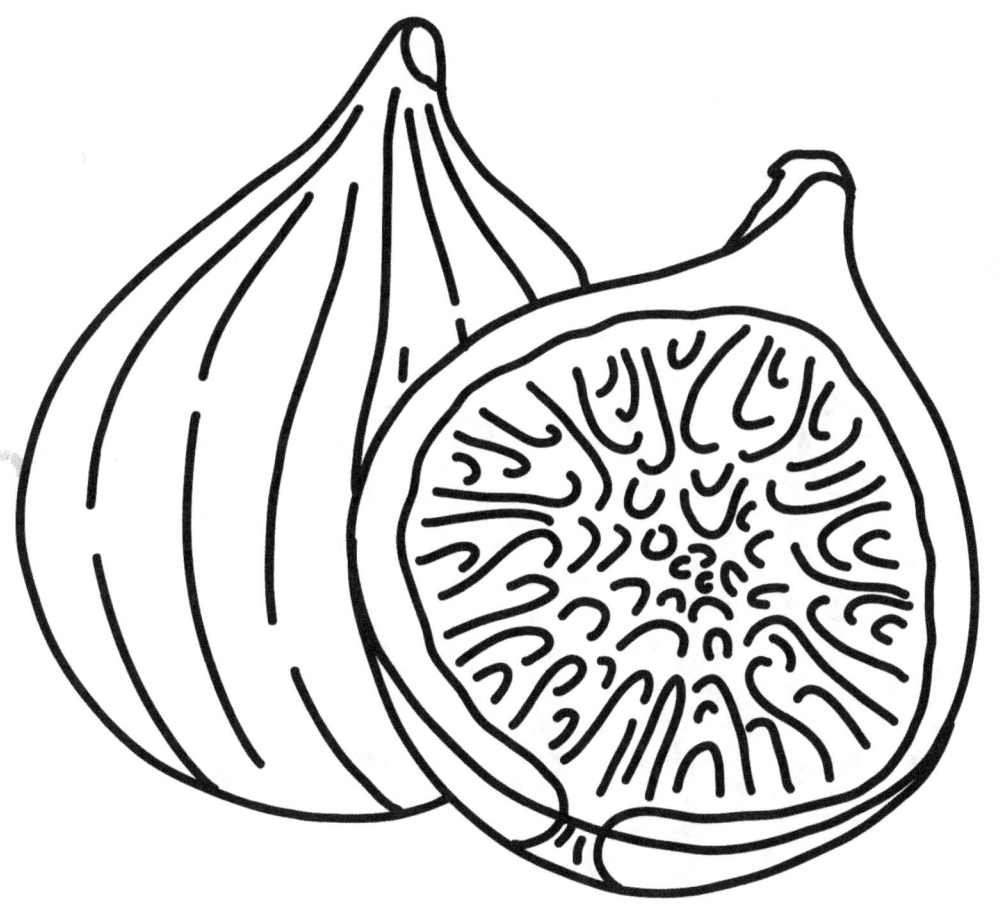

Fig

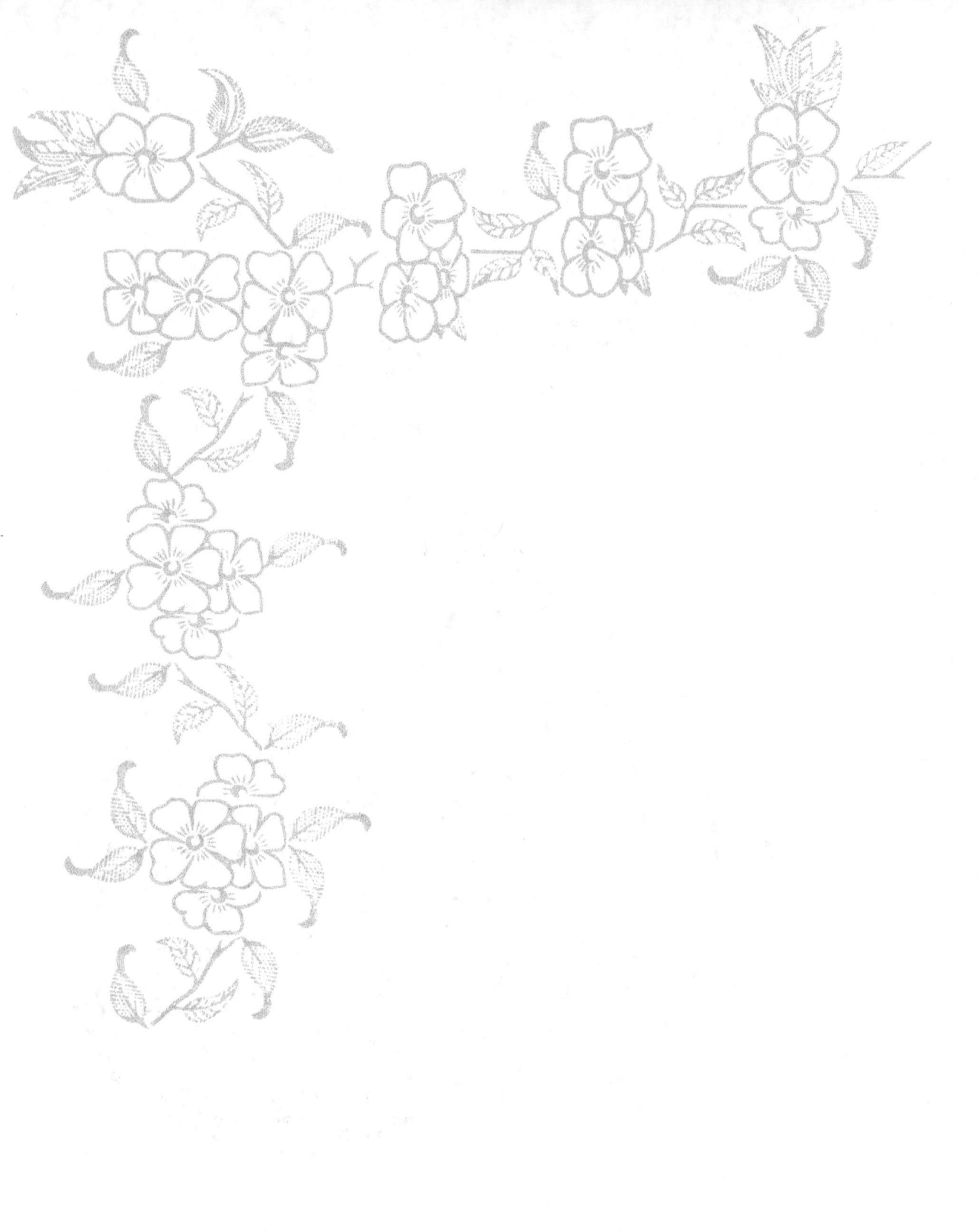

G for

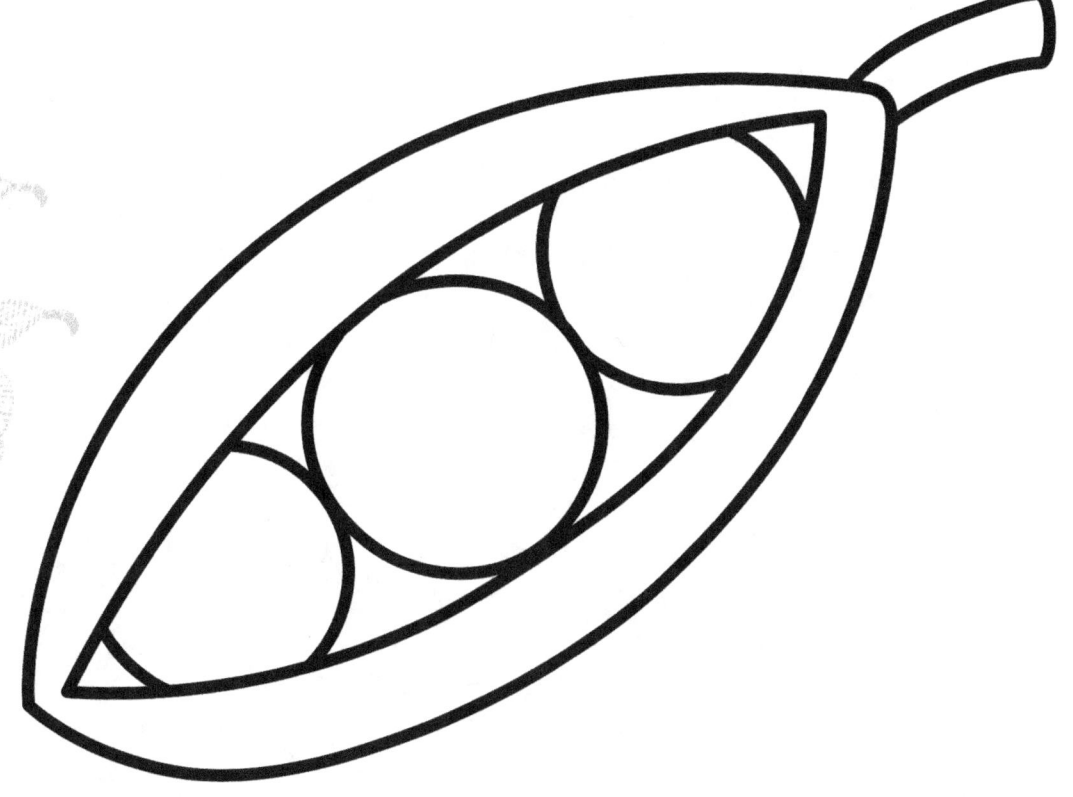

Green Bean

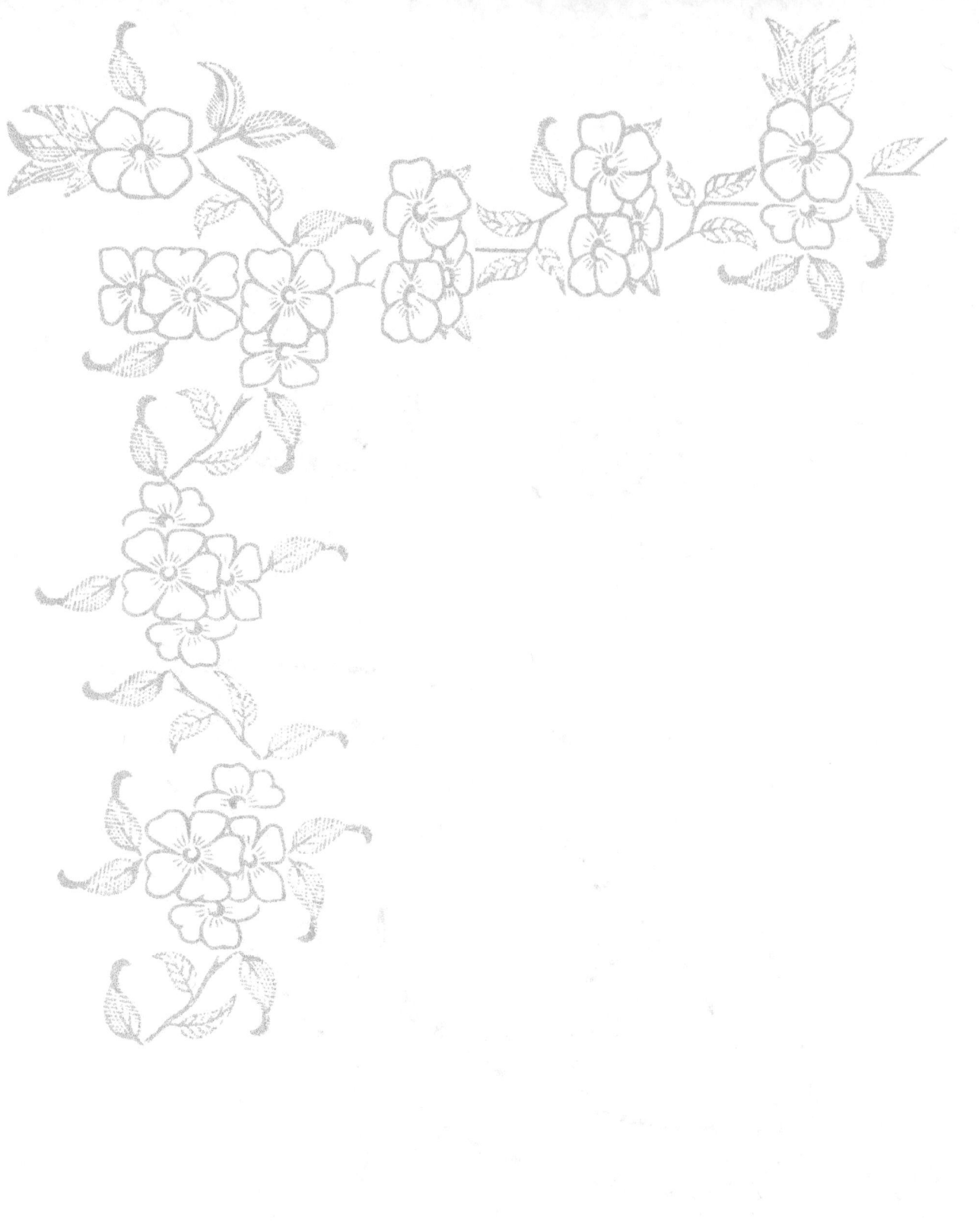

H for

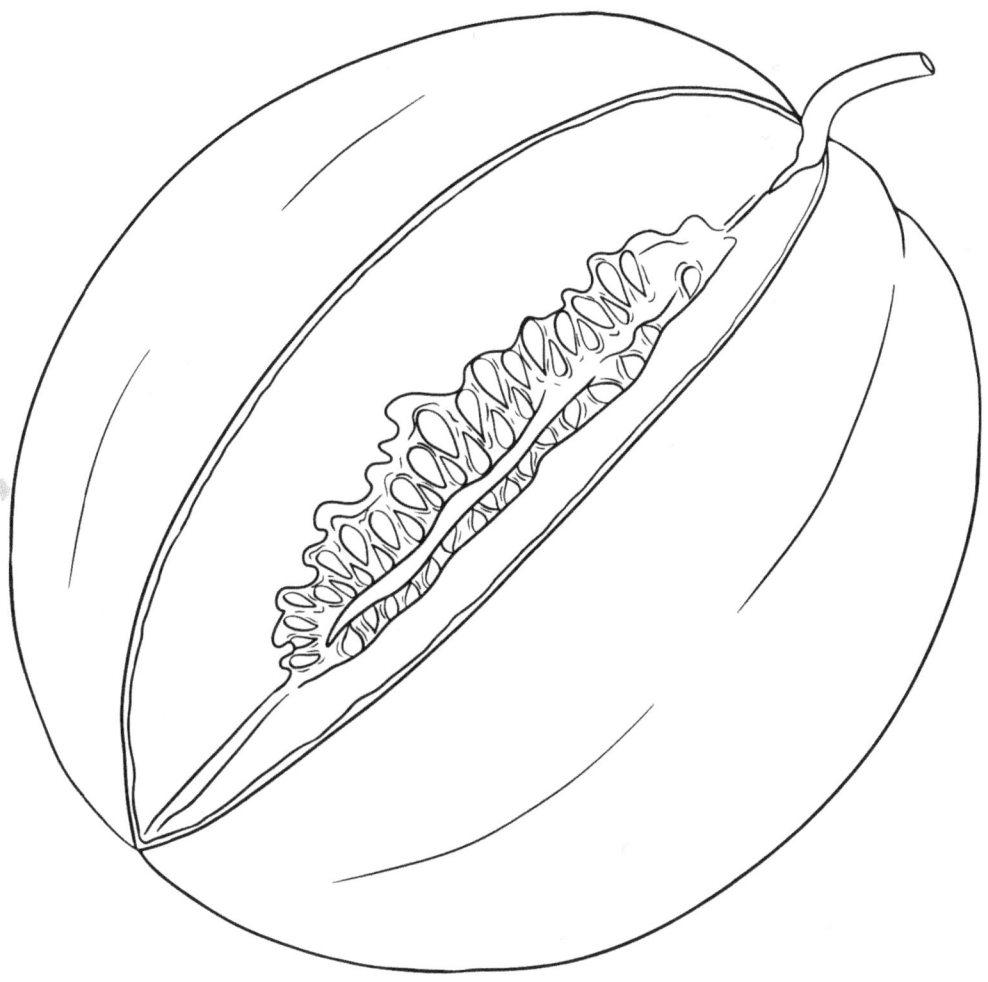

Honeydew

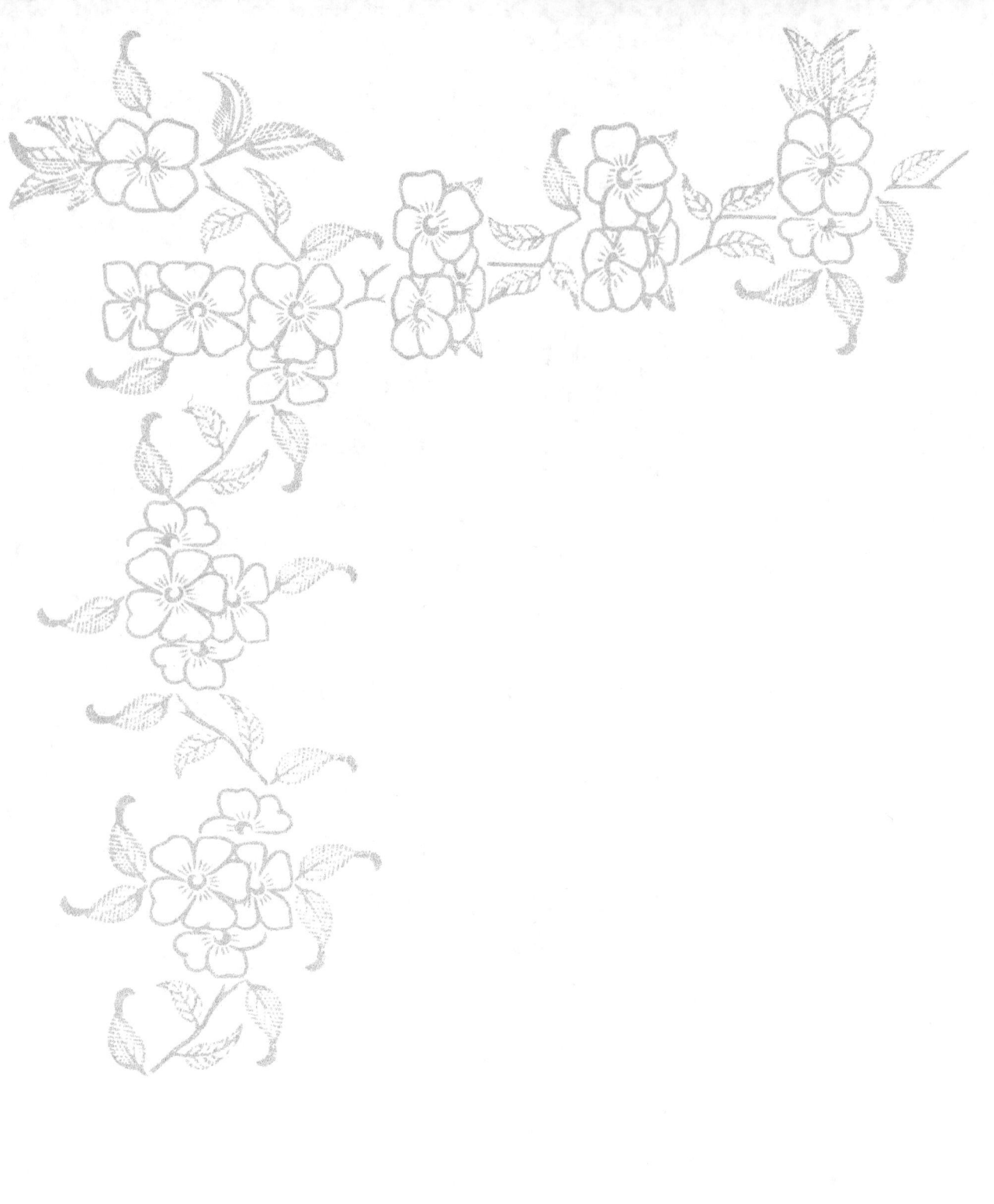

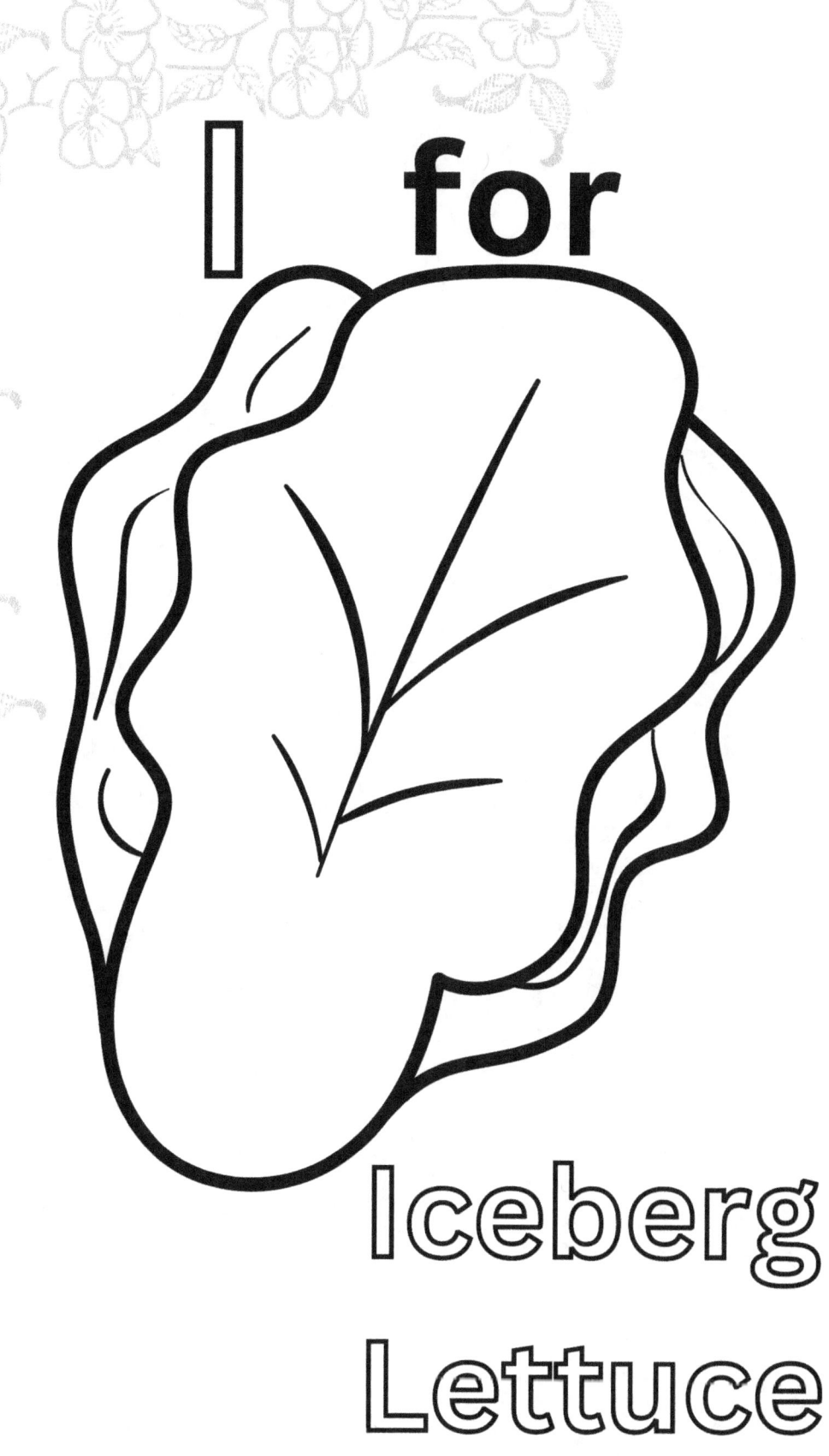

I for Iceberg Lettuce

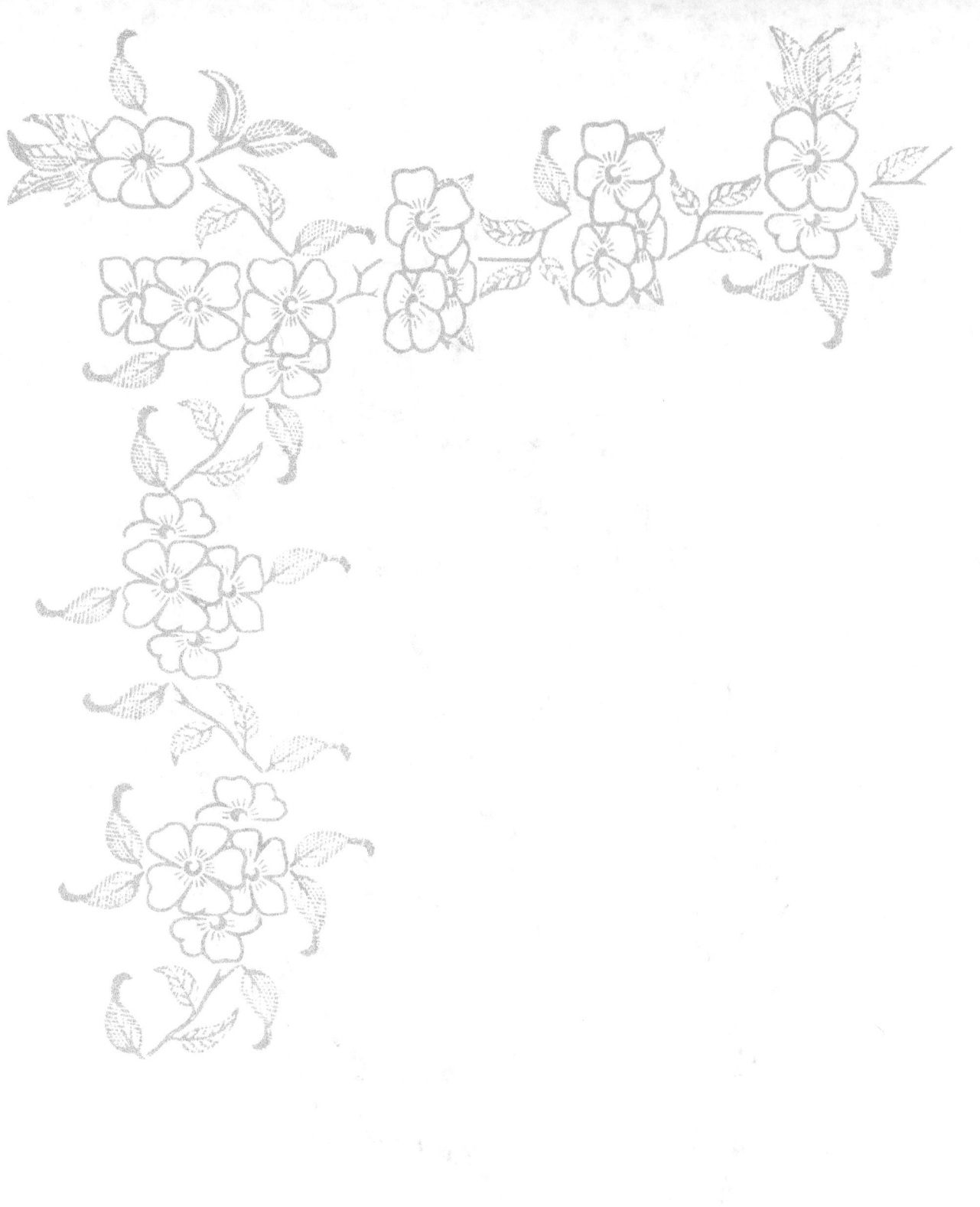

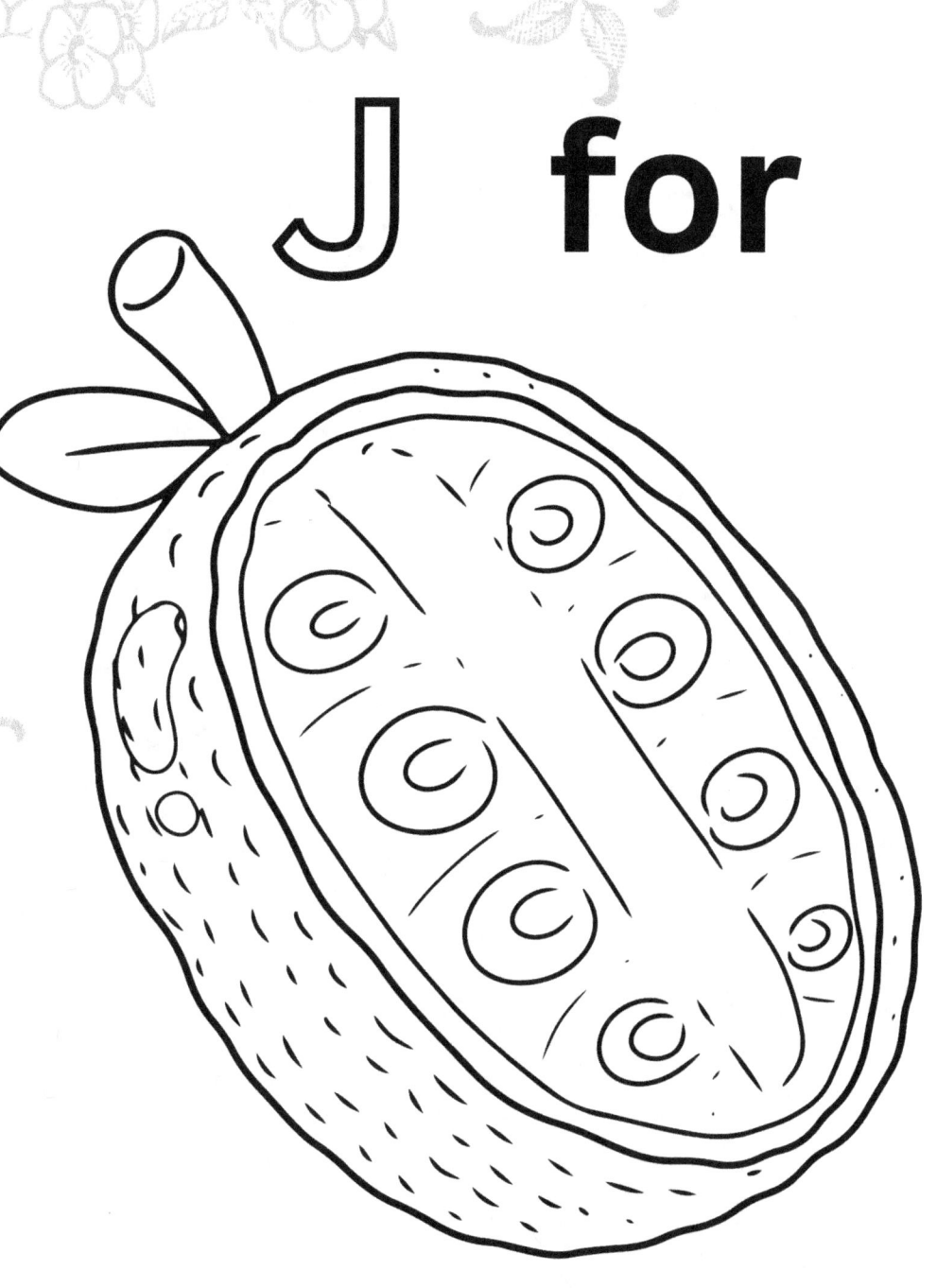

J for
Jackfruit

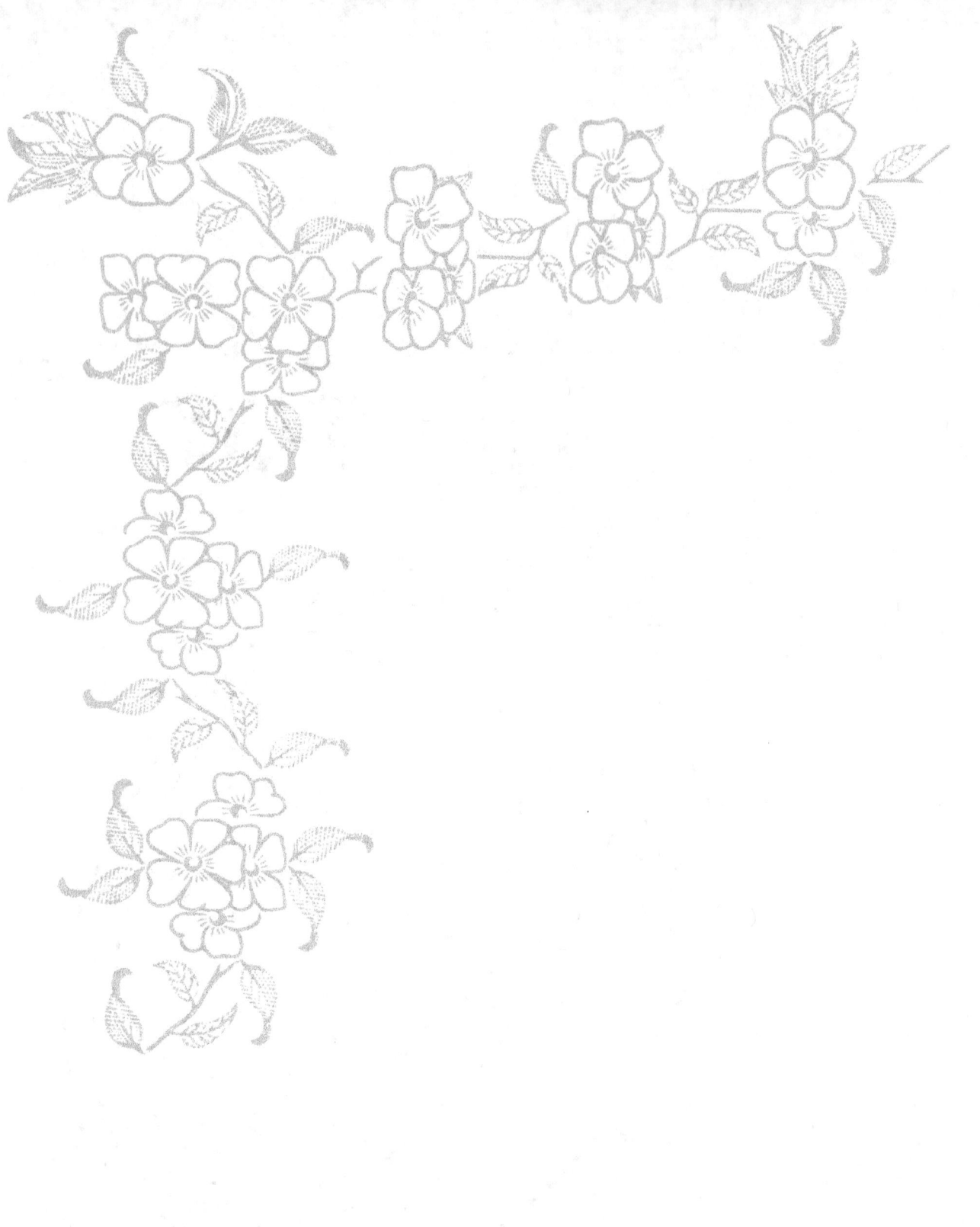

K for

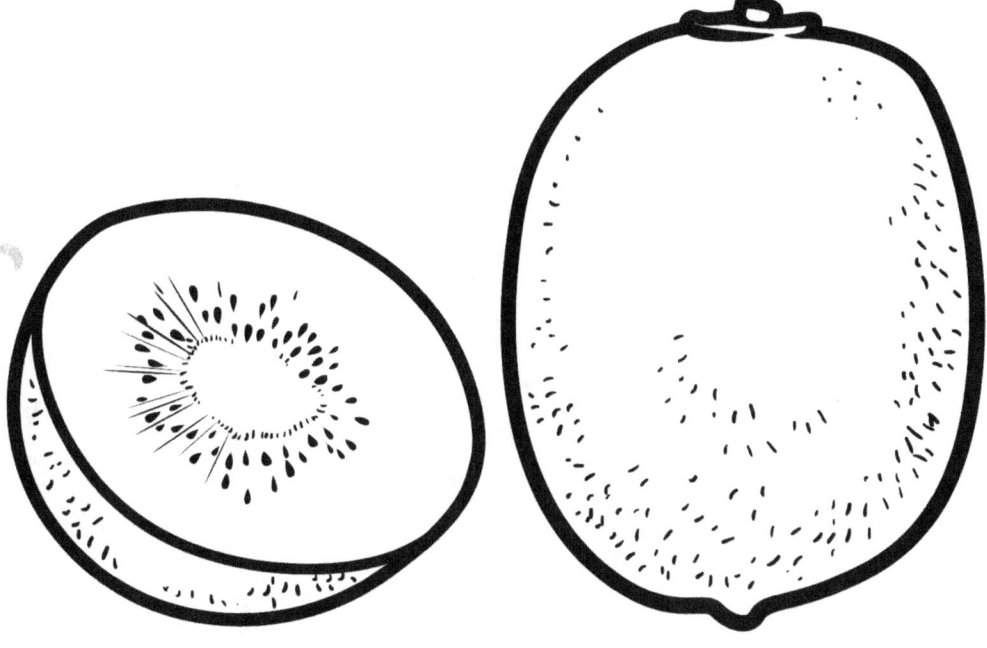

Kiwi

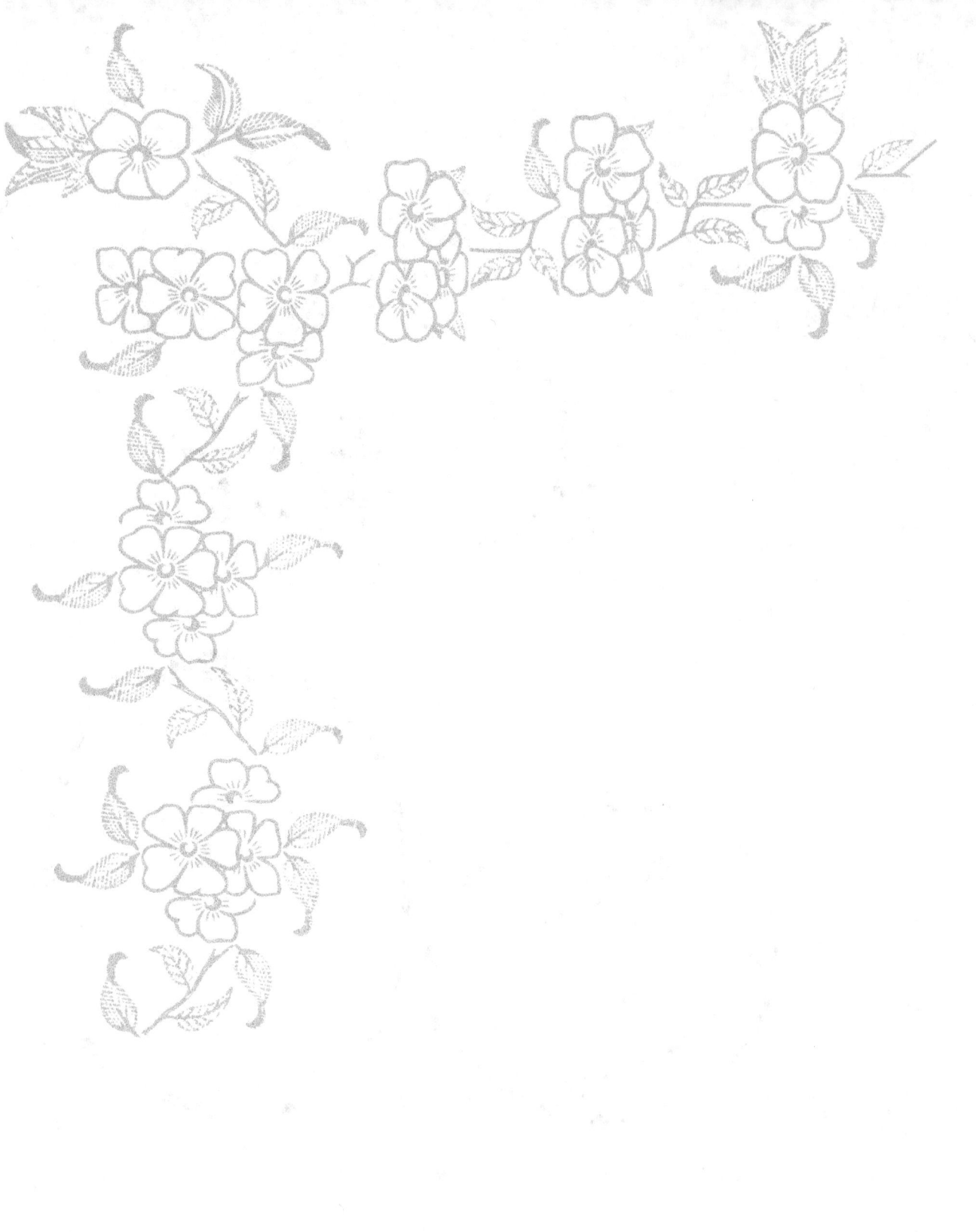

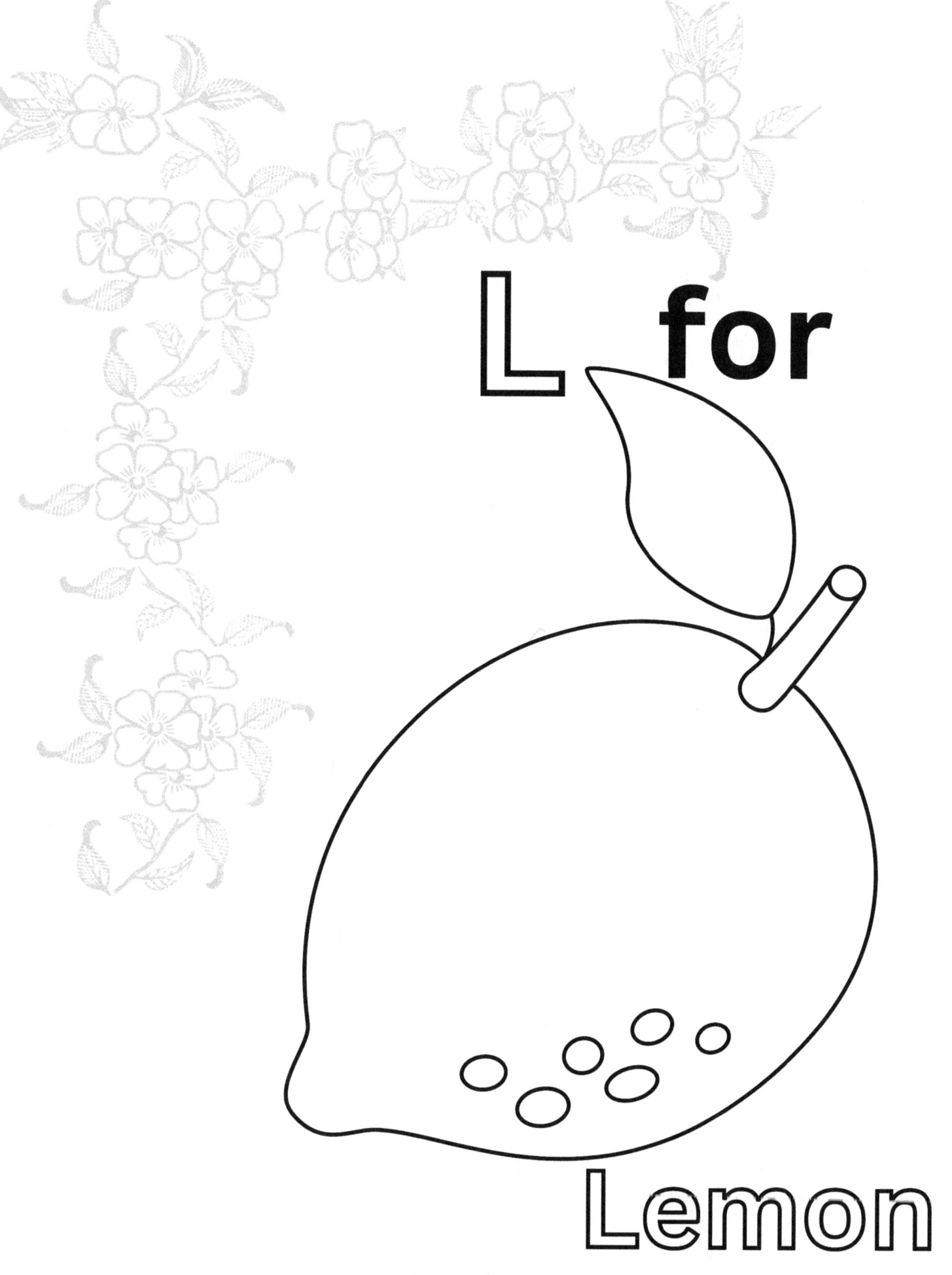

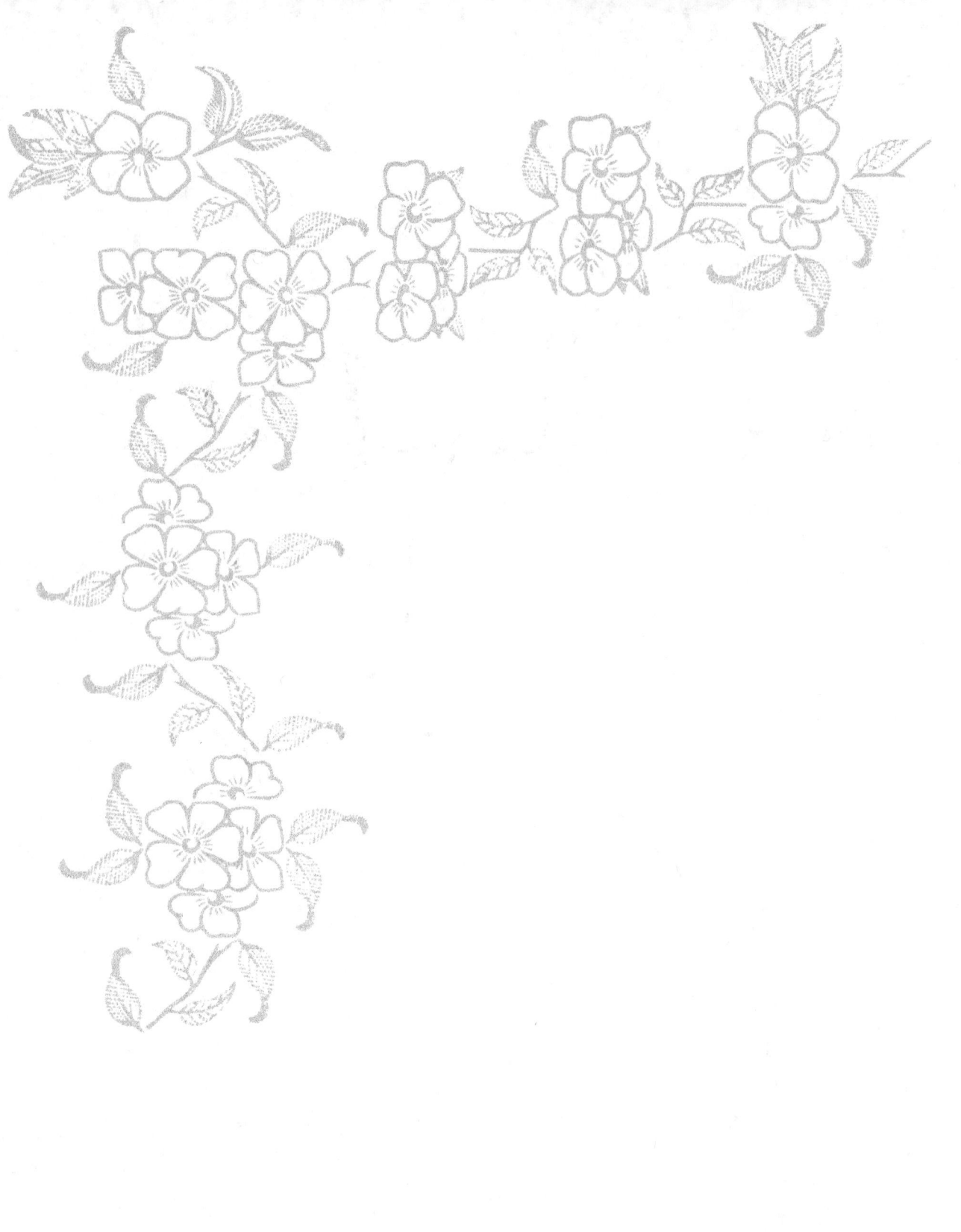

M for Mushroom

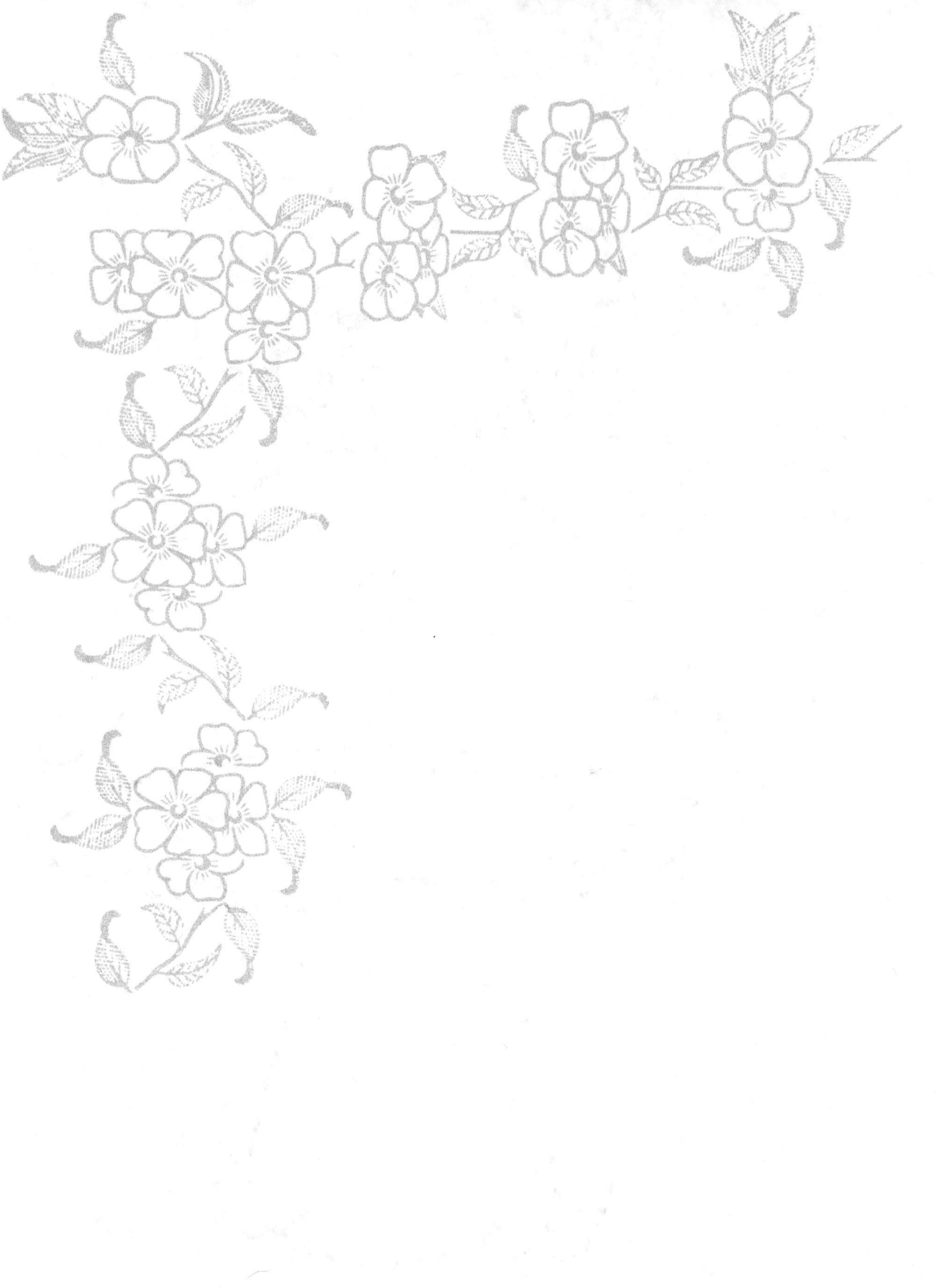

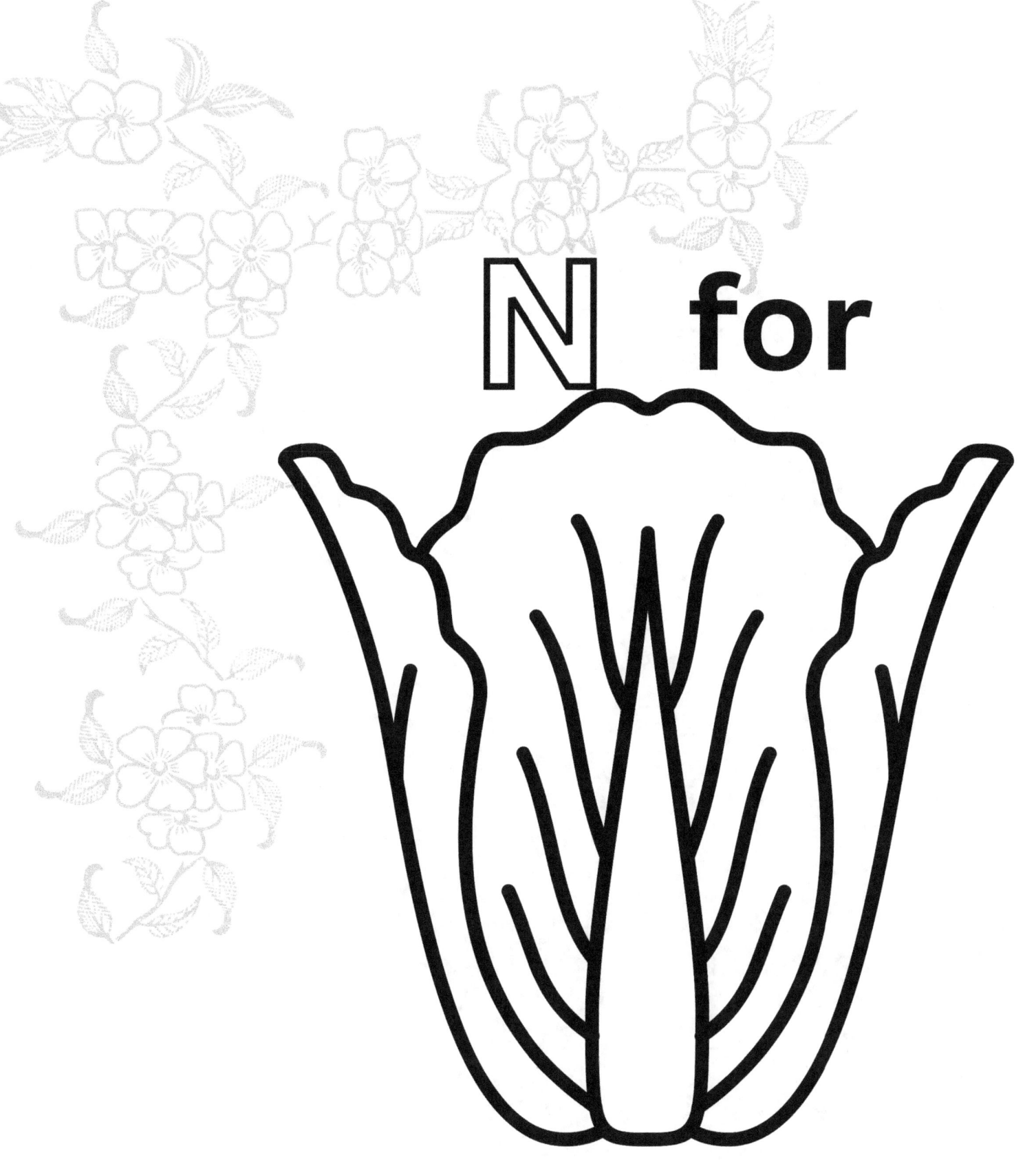

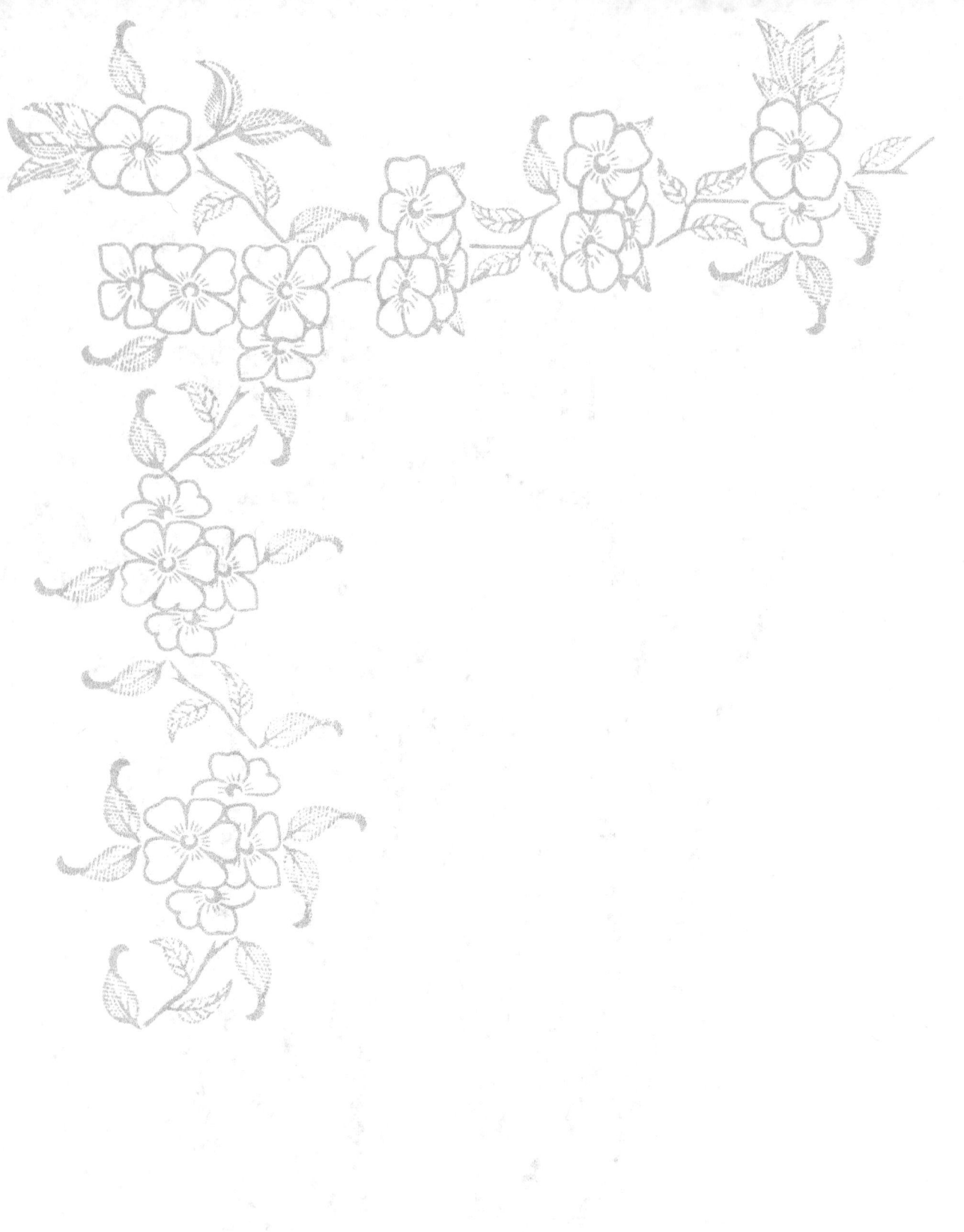

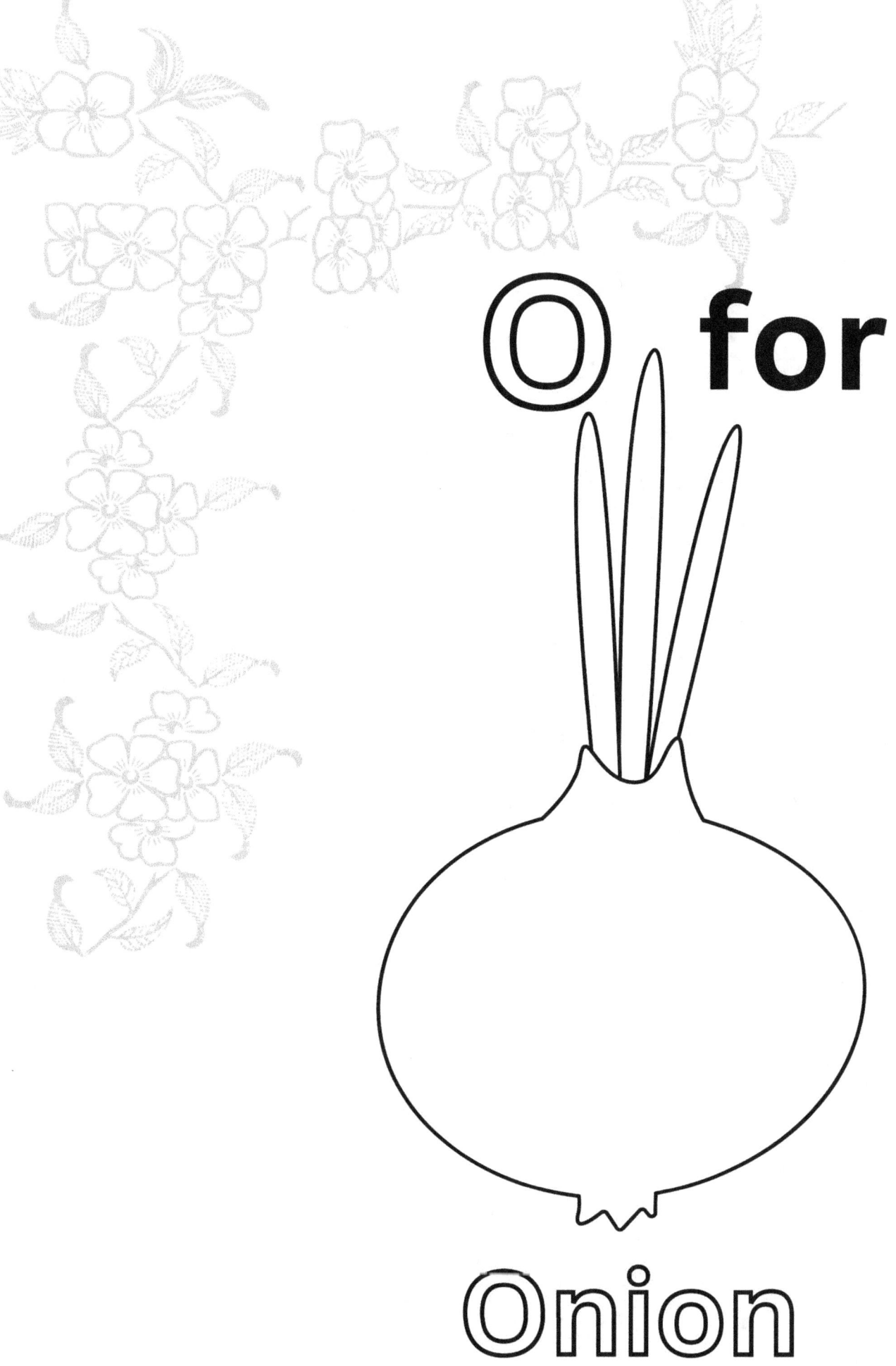

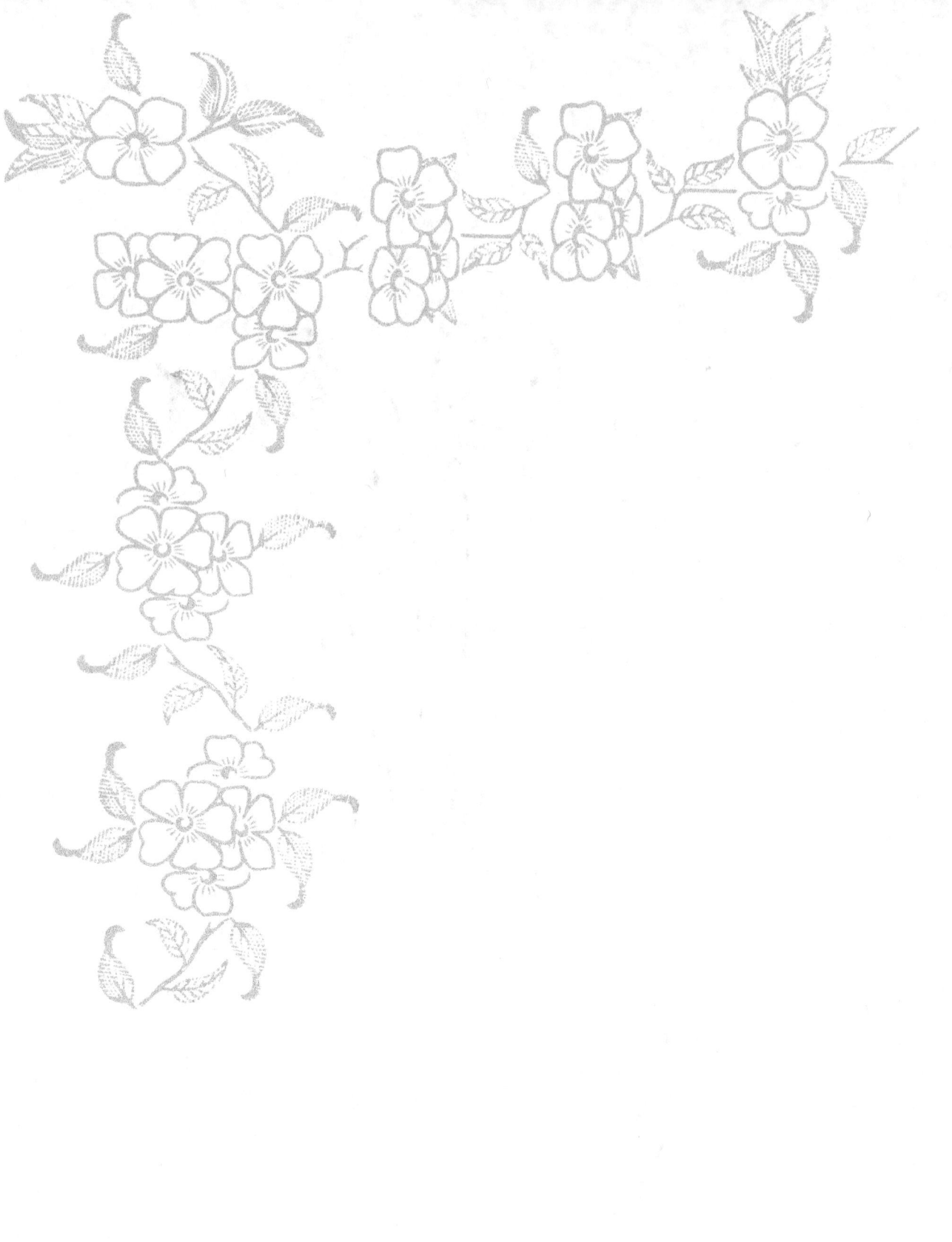

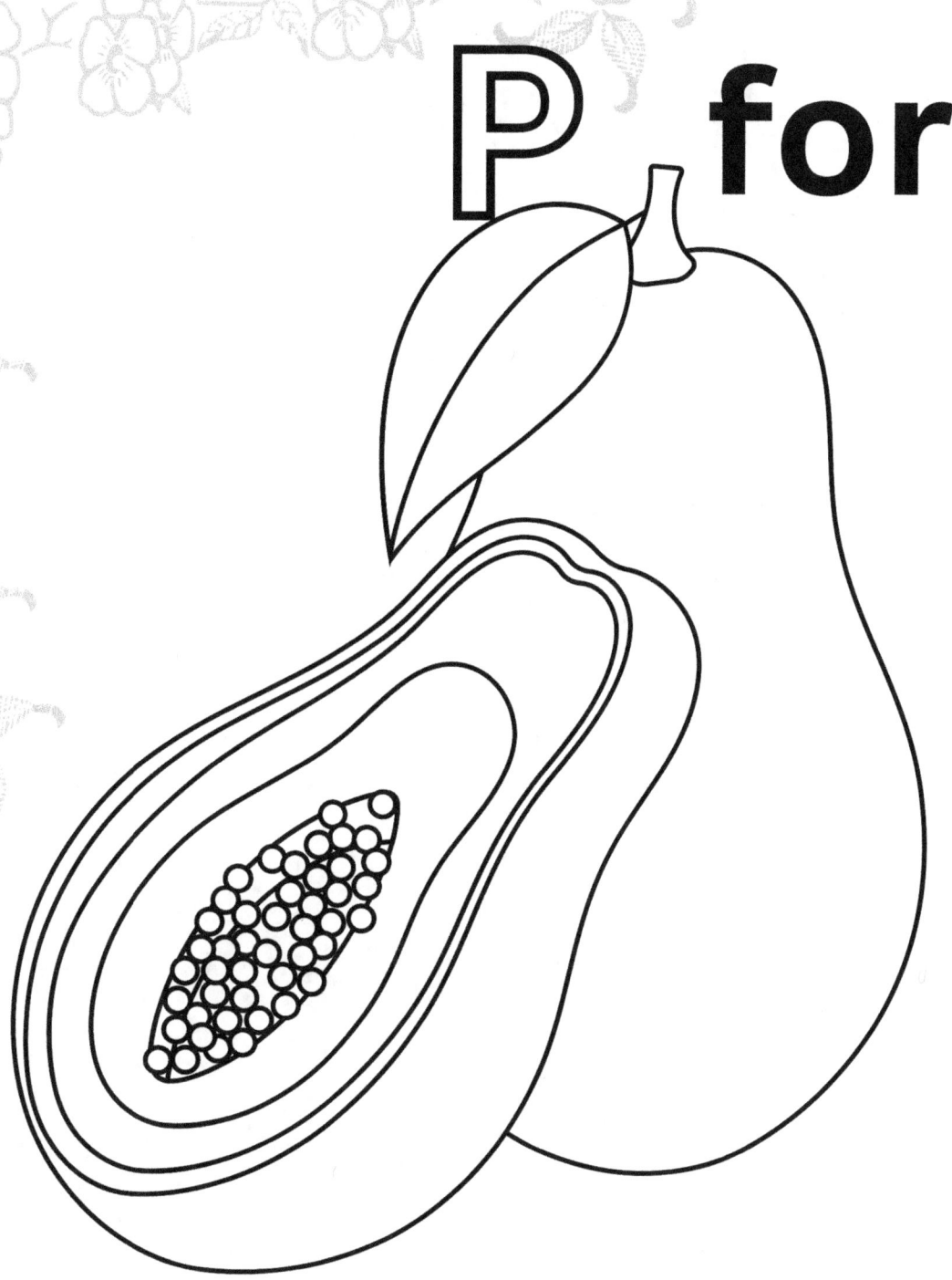

P for

Papaya

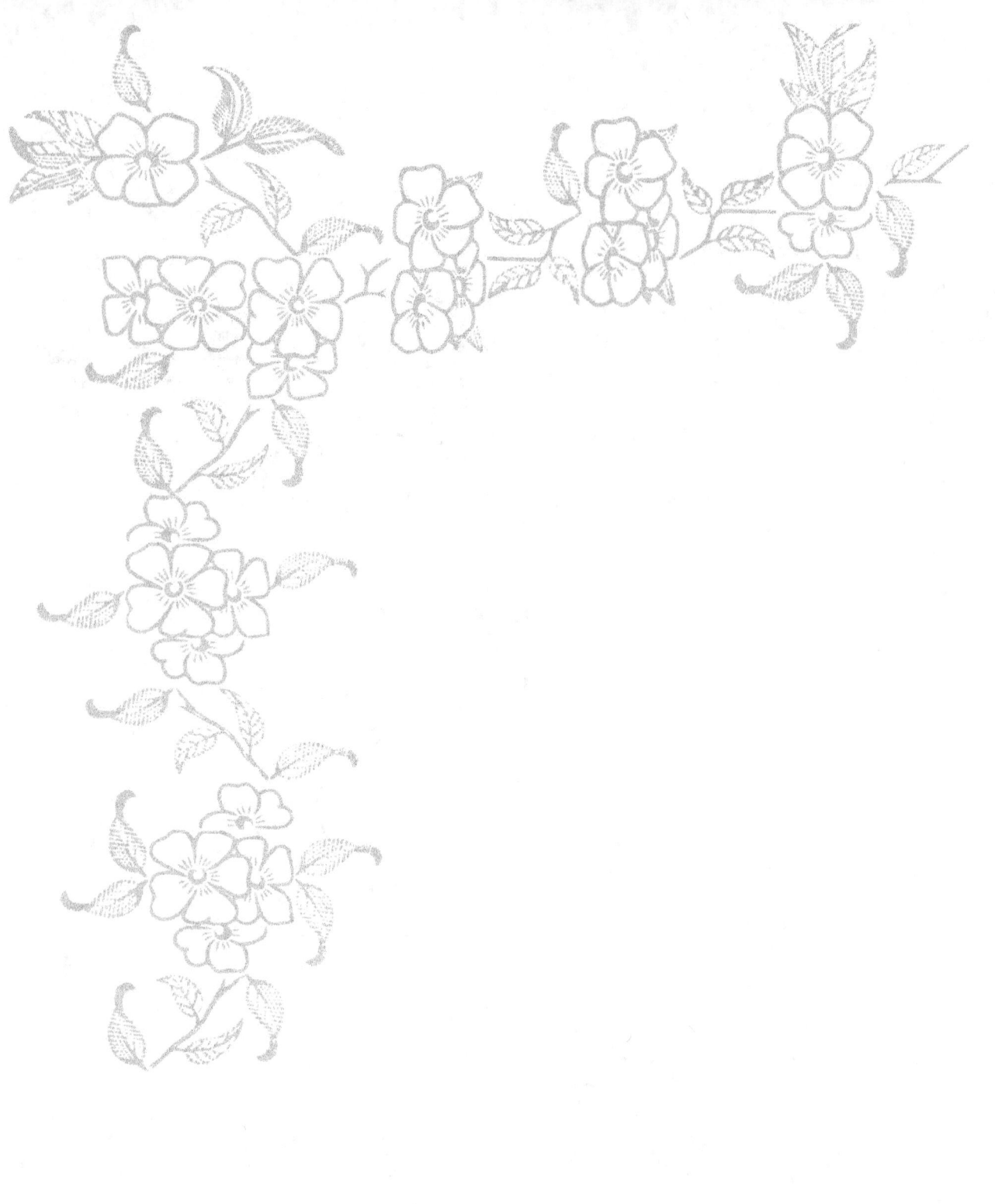

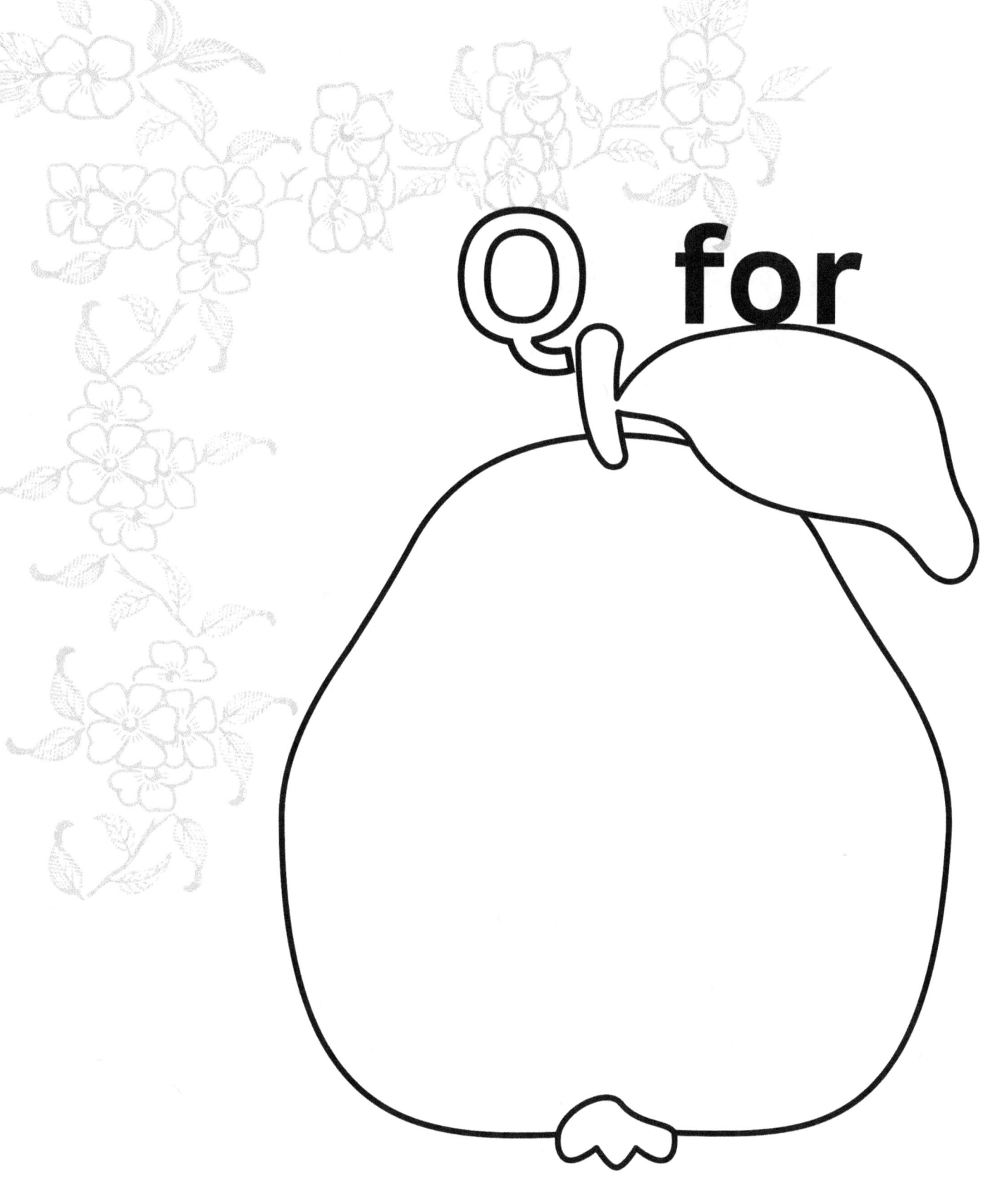

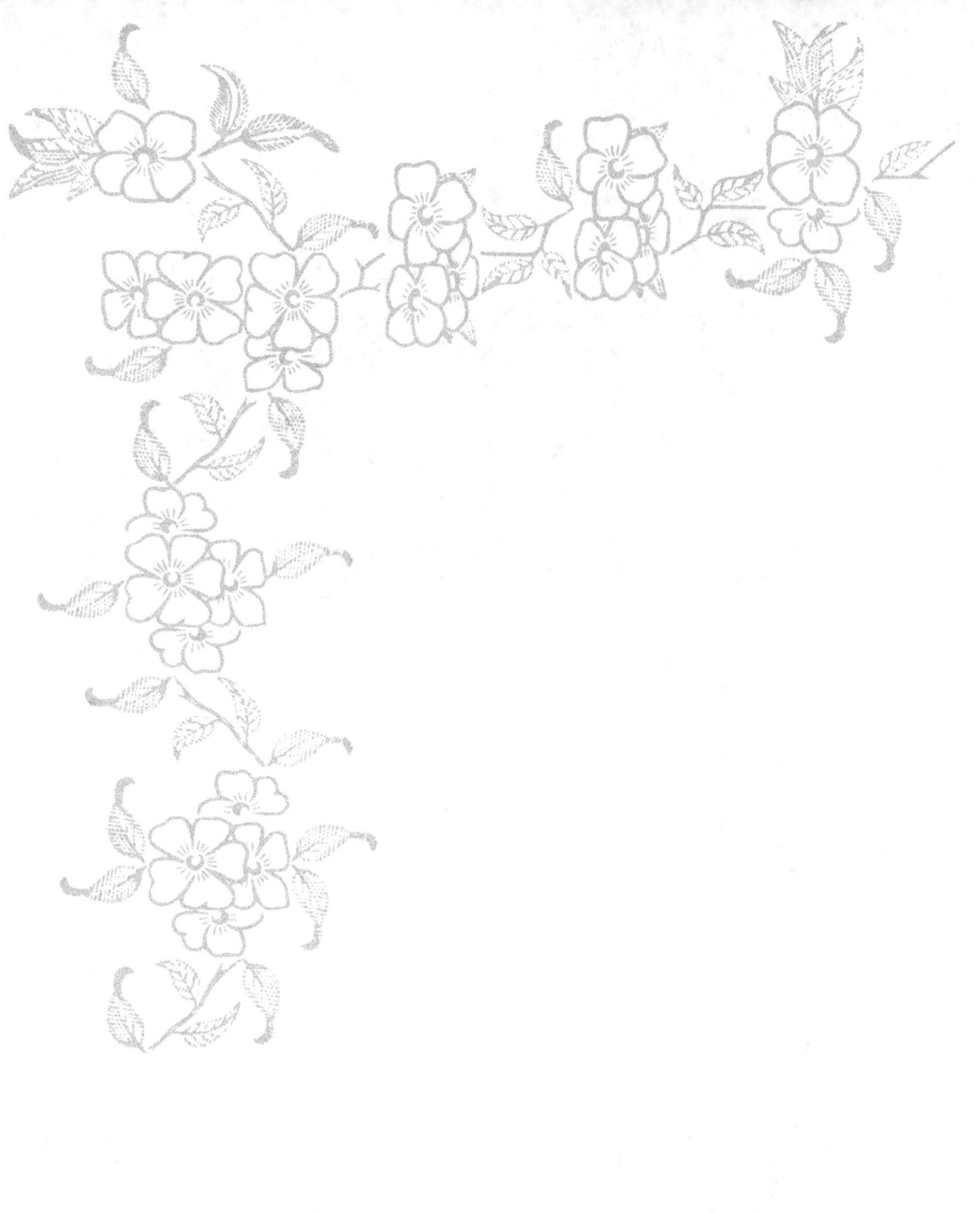

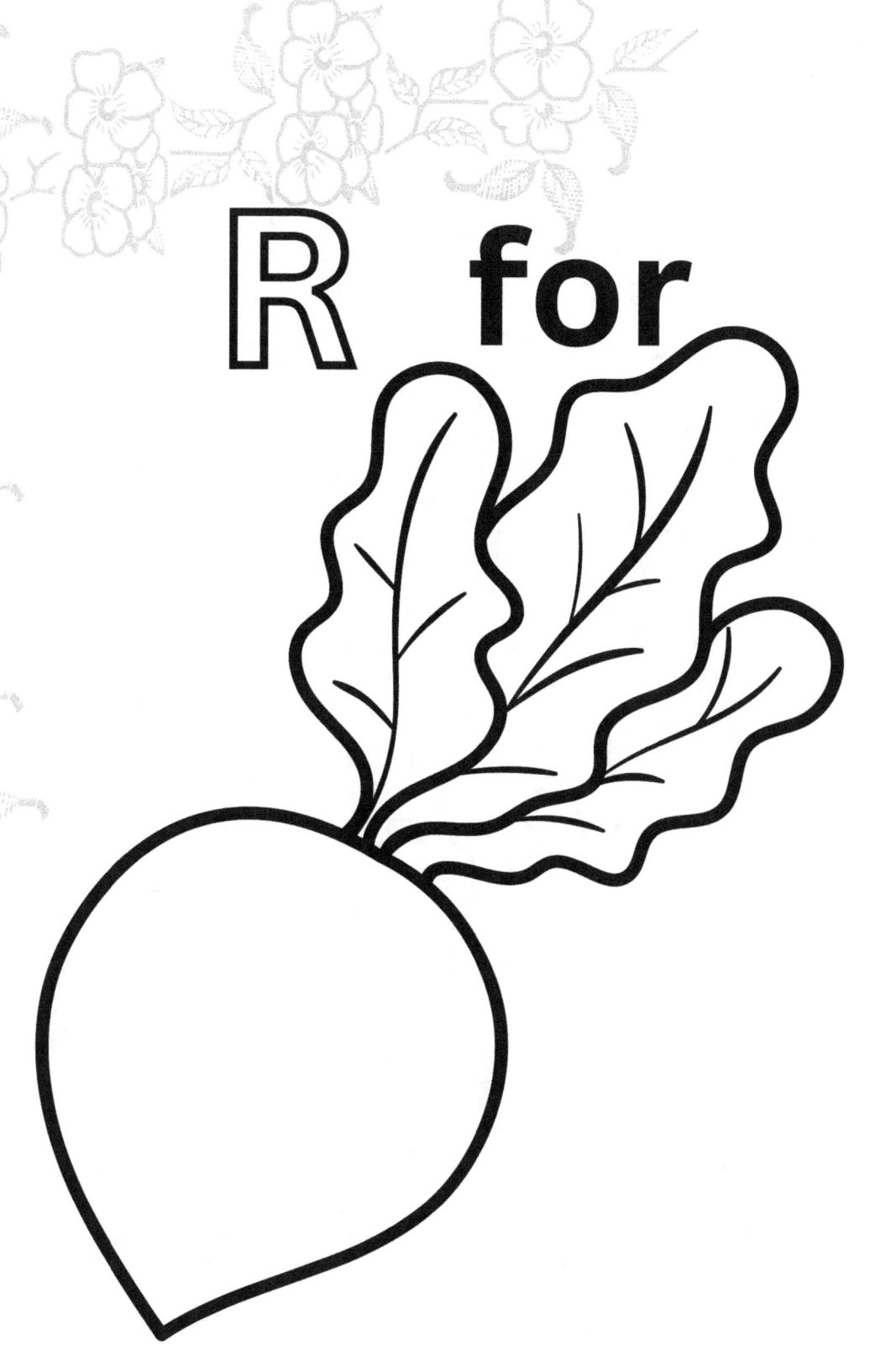

R for

Radish

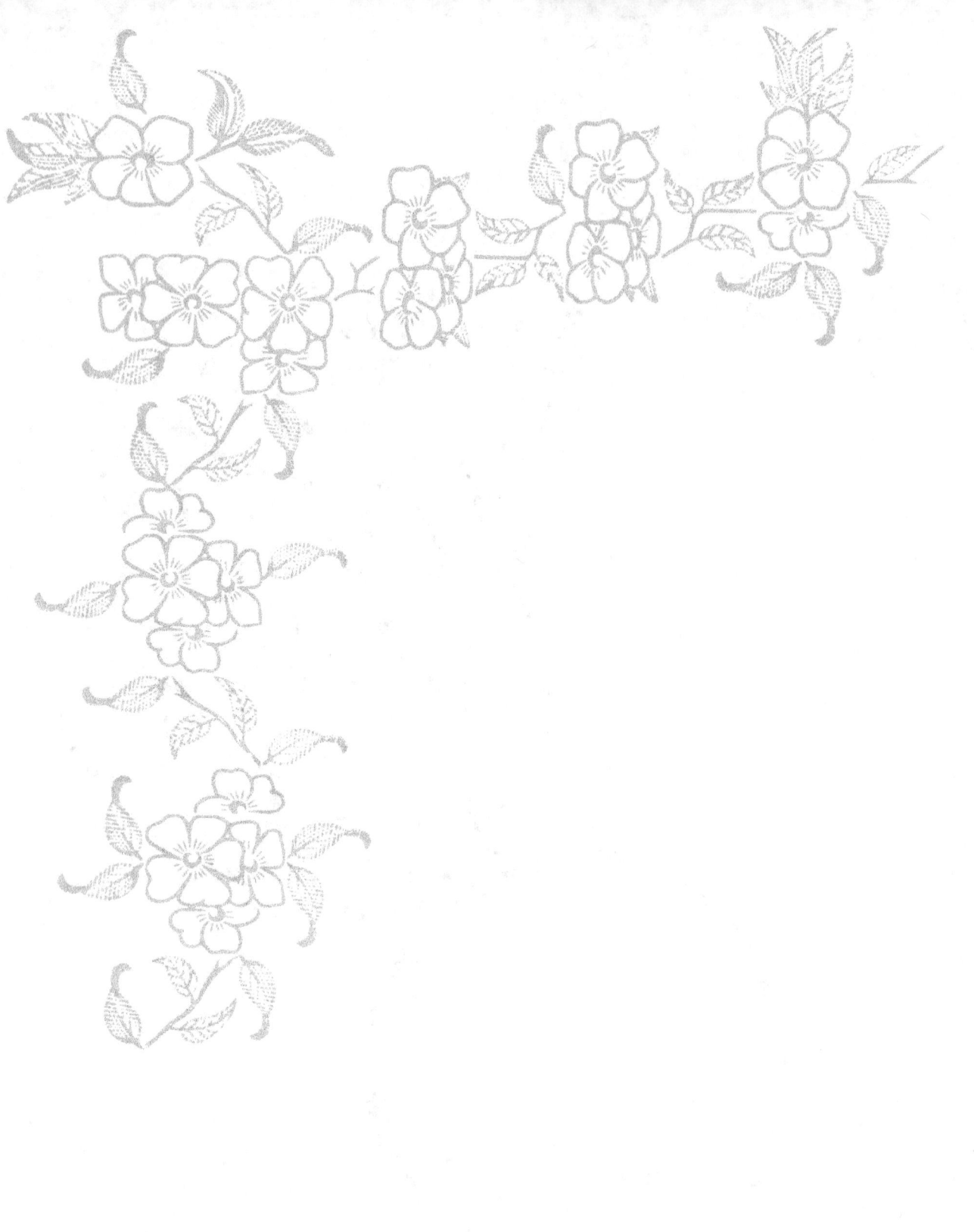

S for

Strawberry

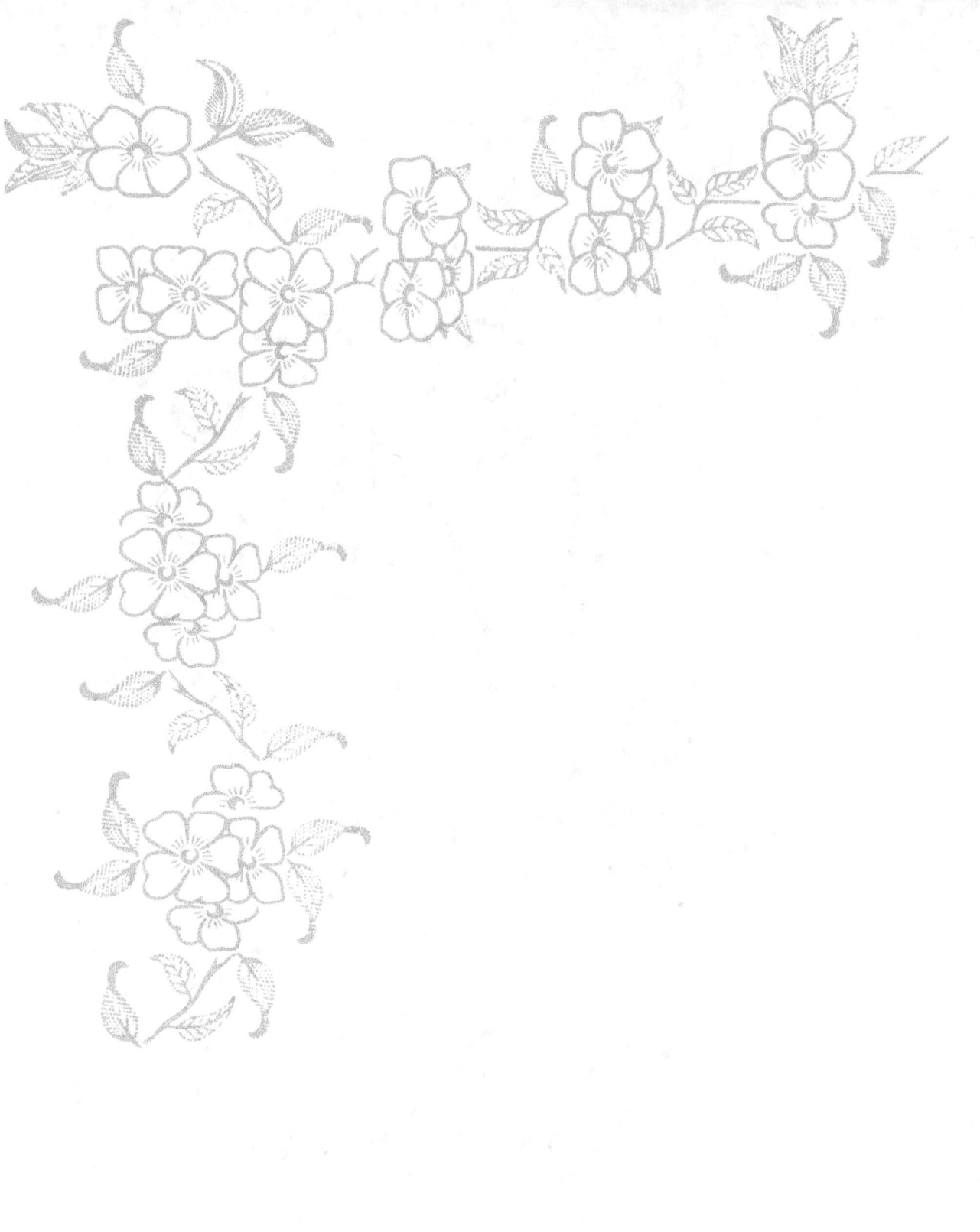

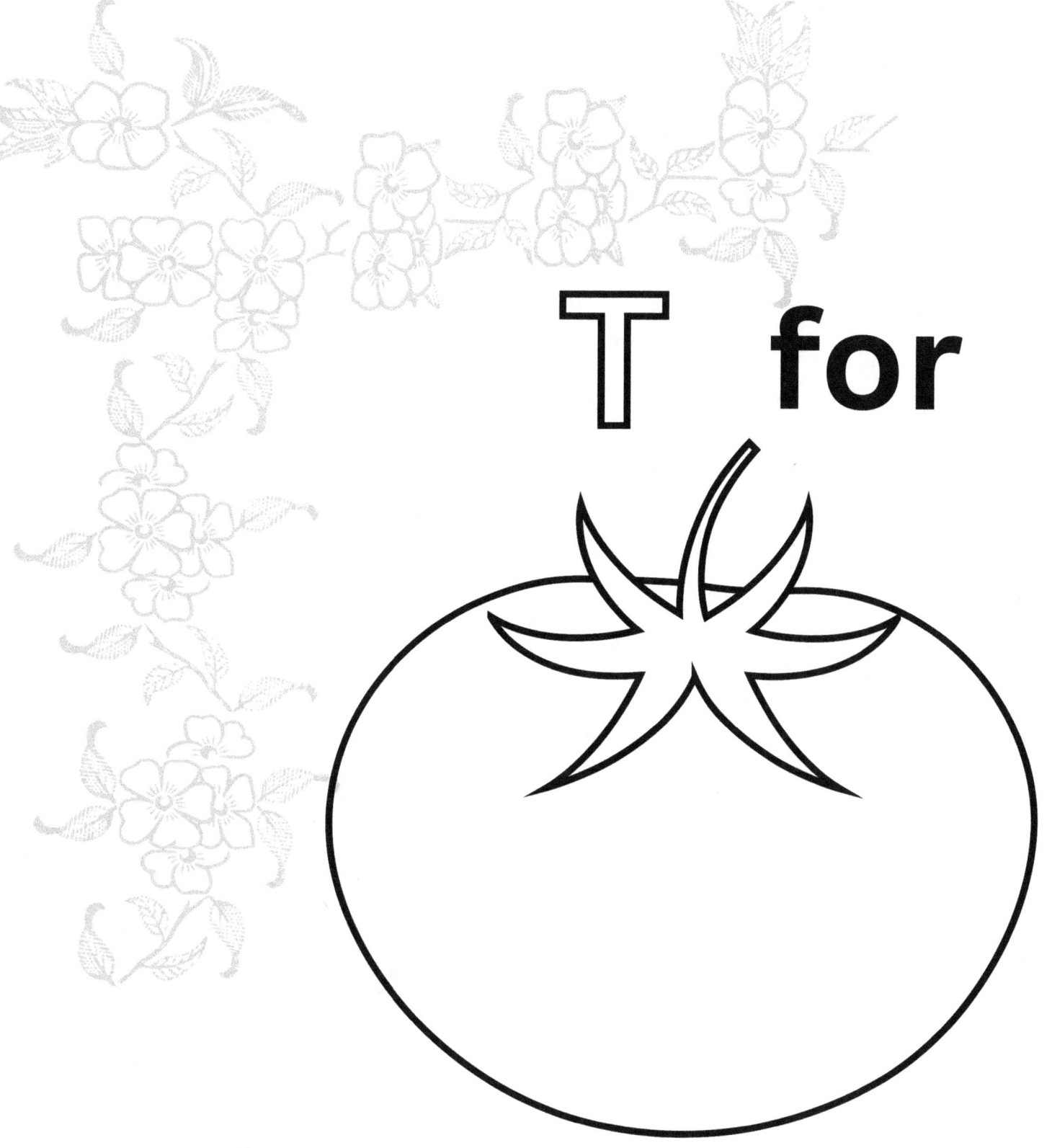

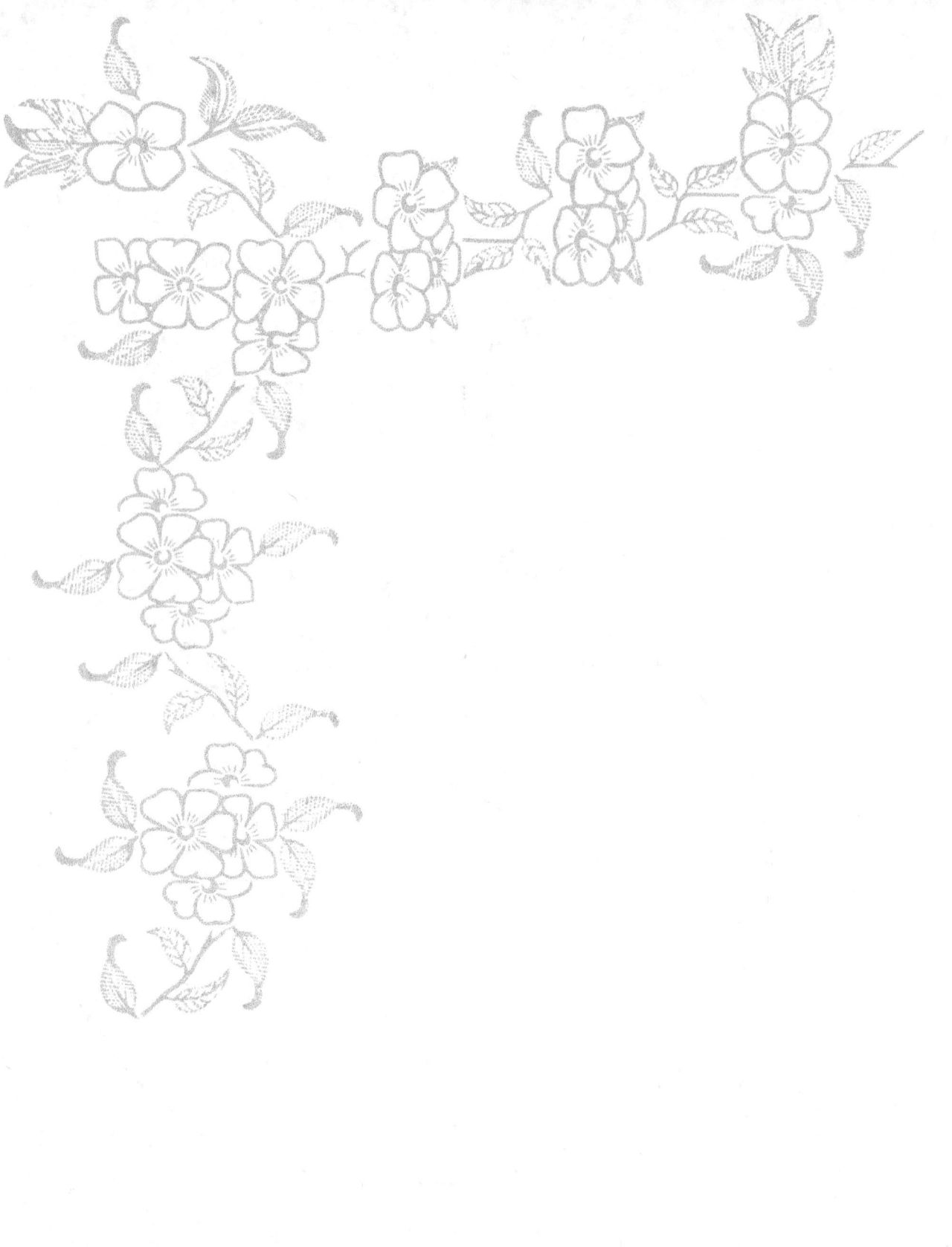

U for

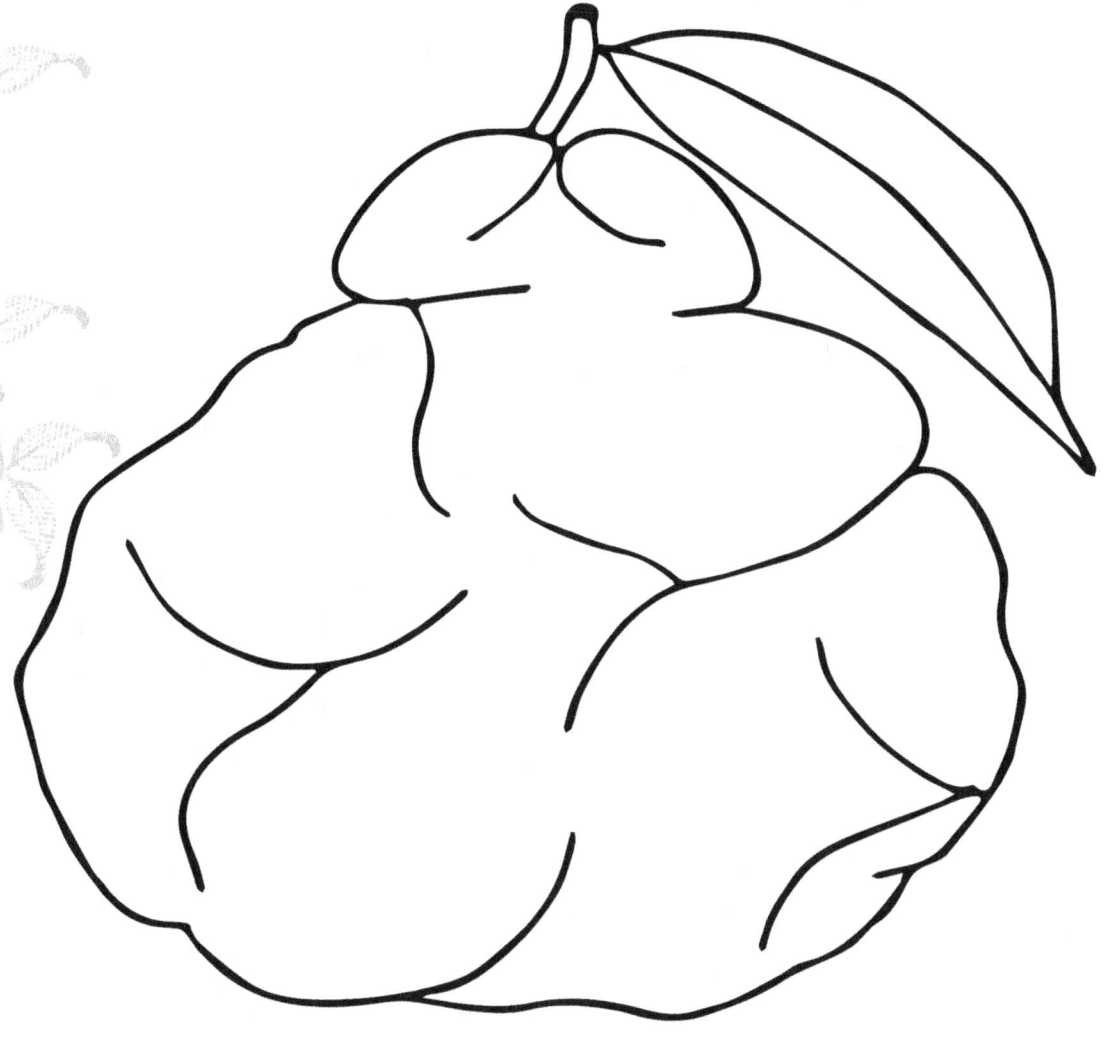

Ugli Fruit

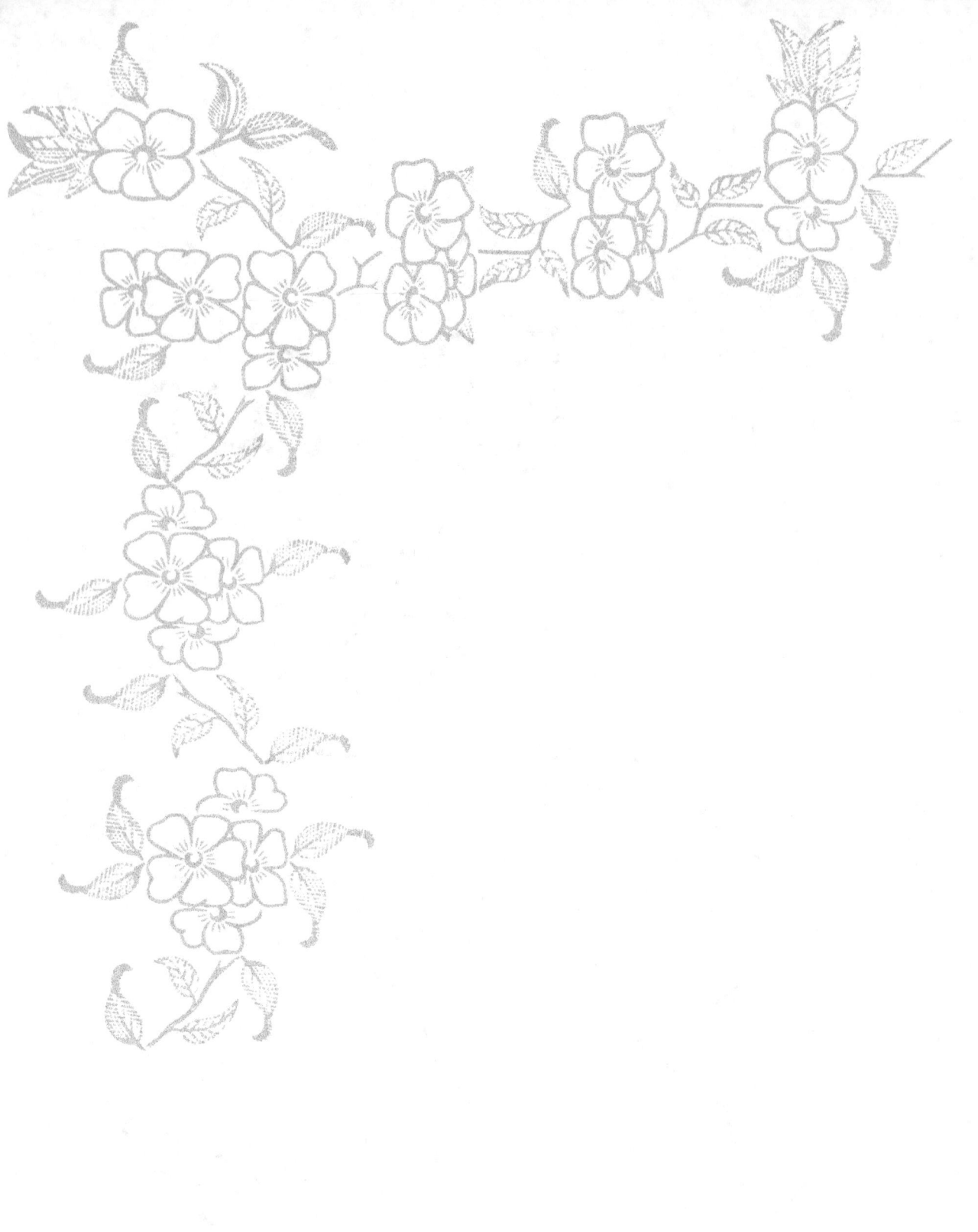

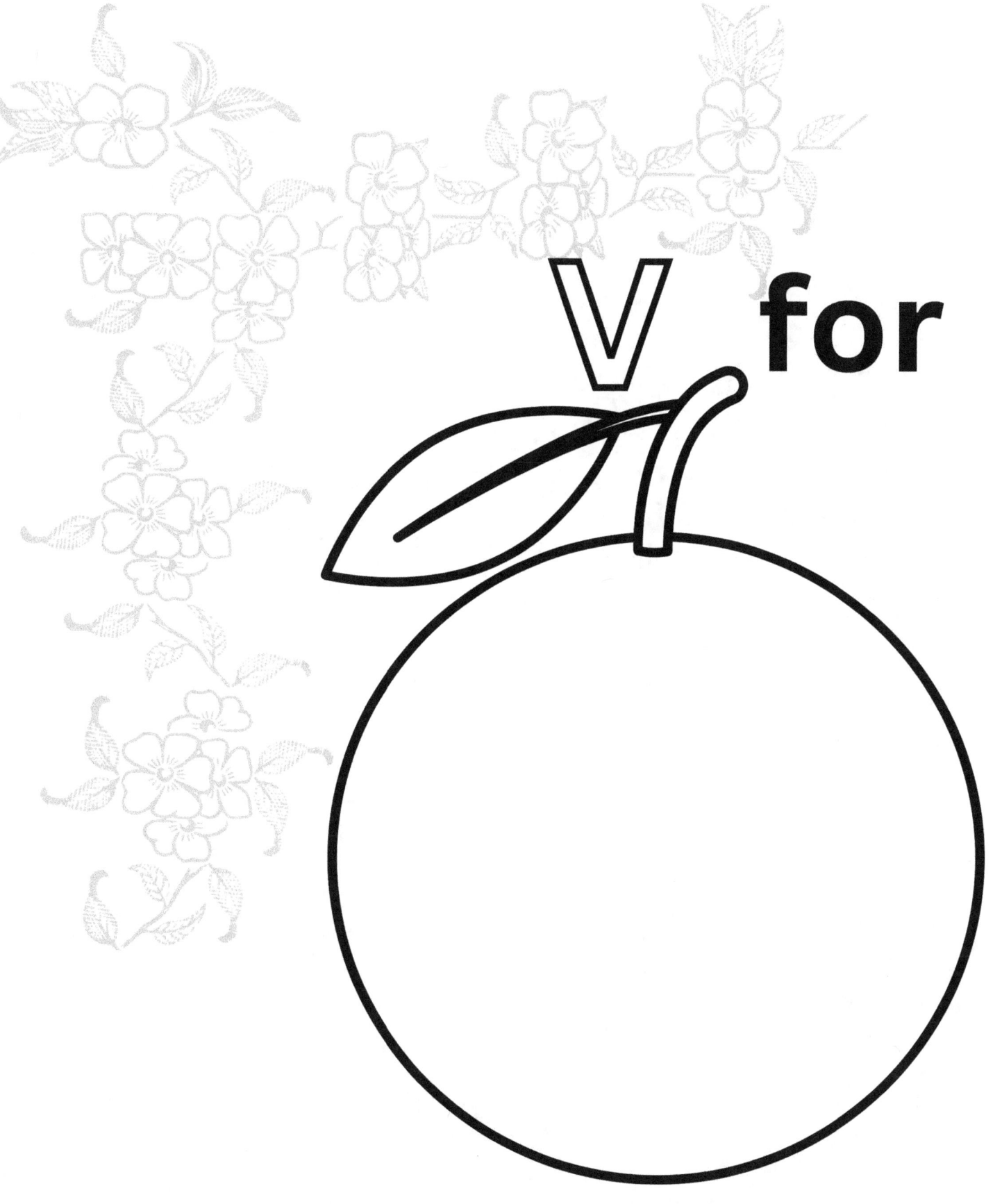

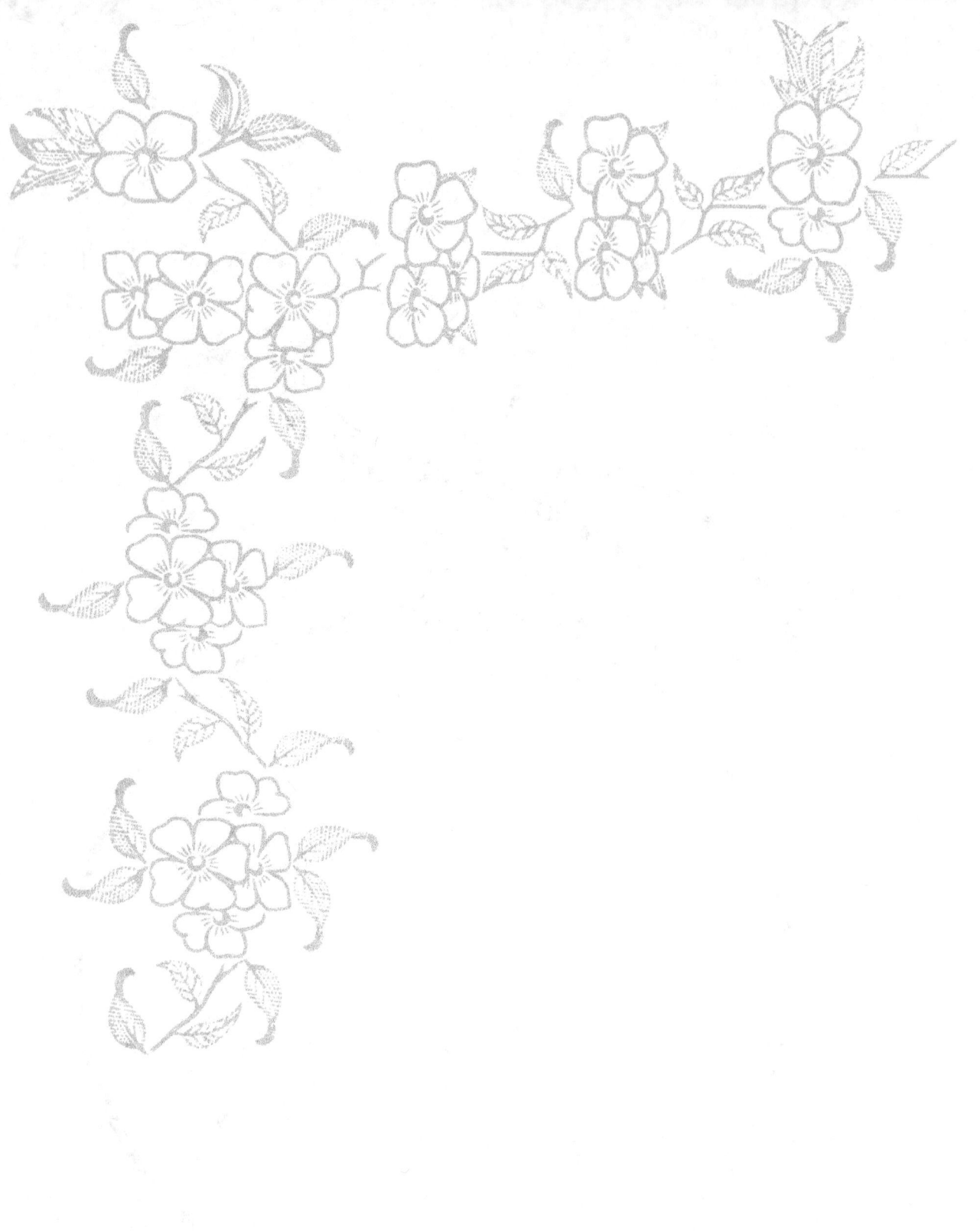

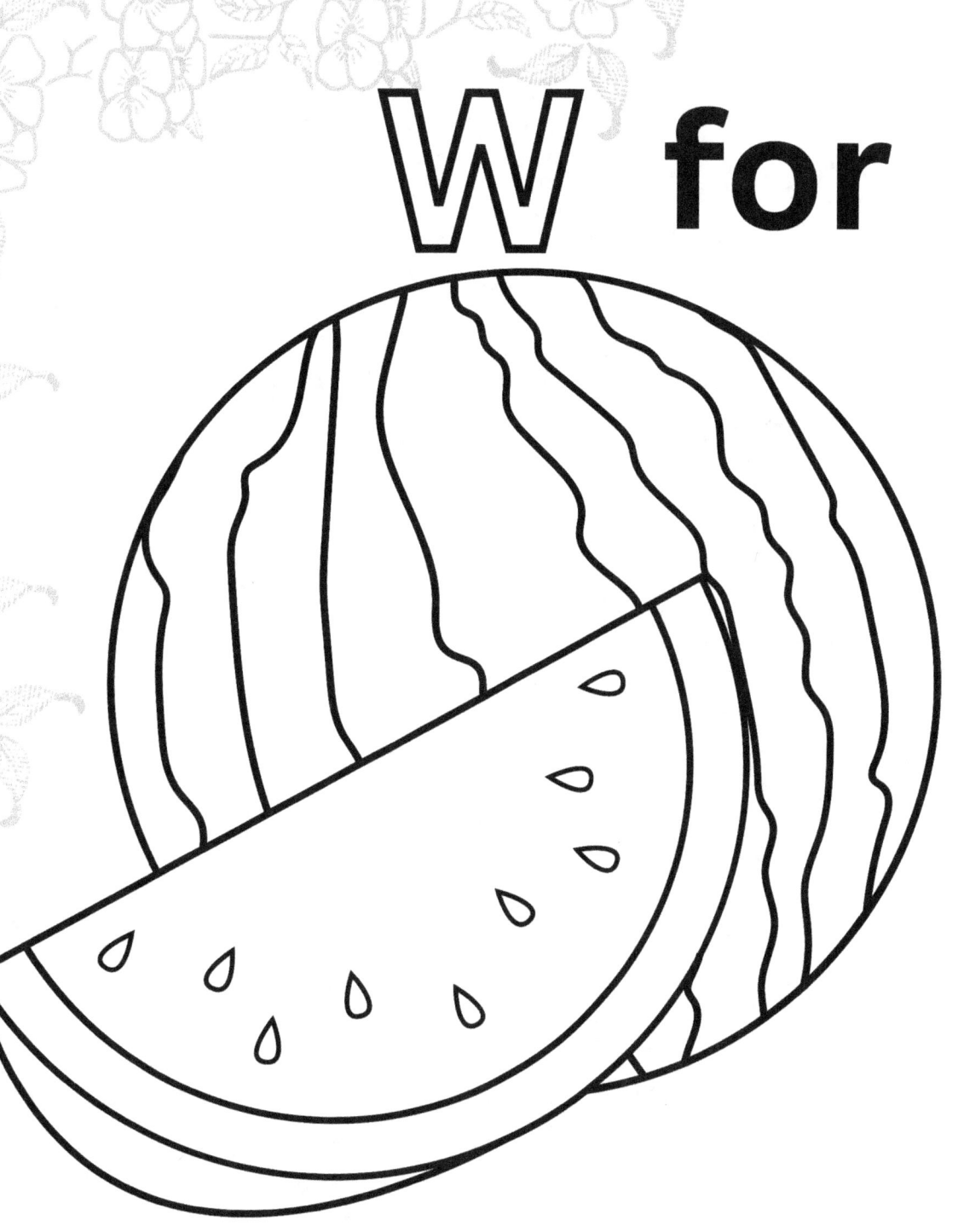

W for

Watermelon

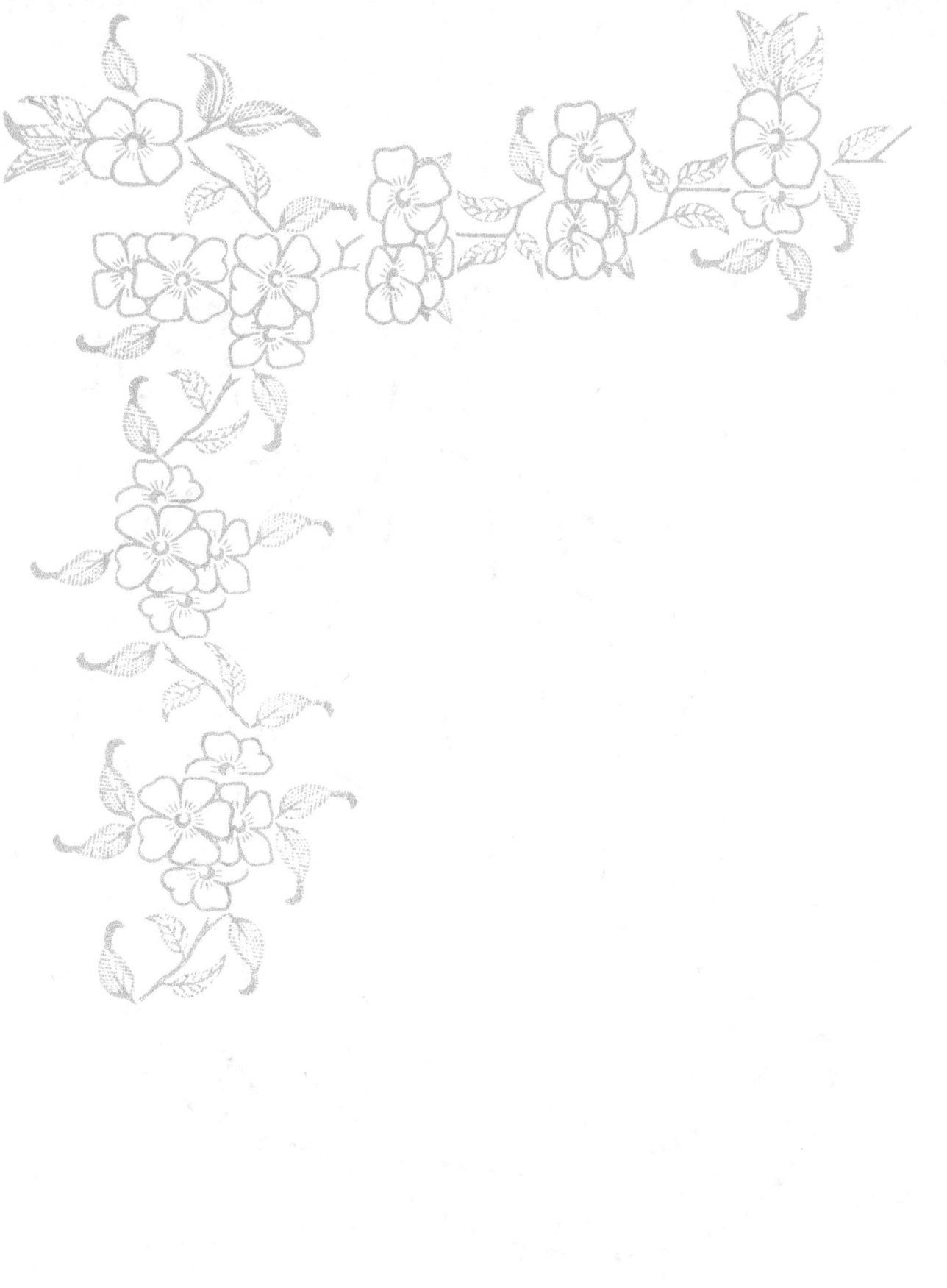

X for

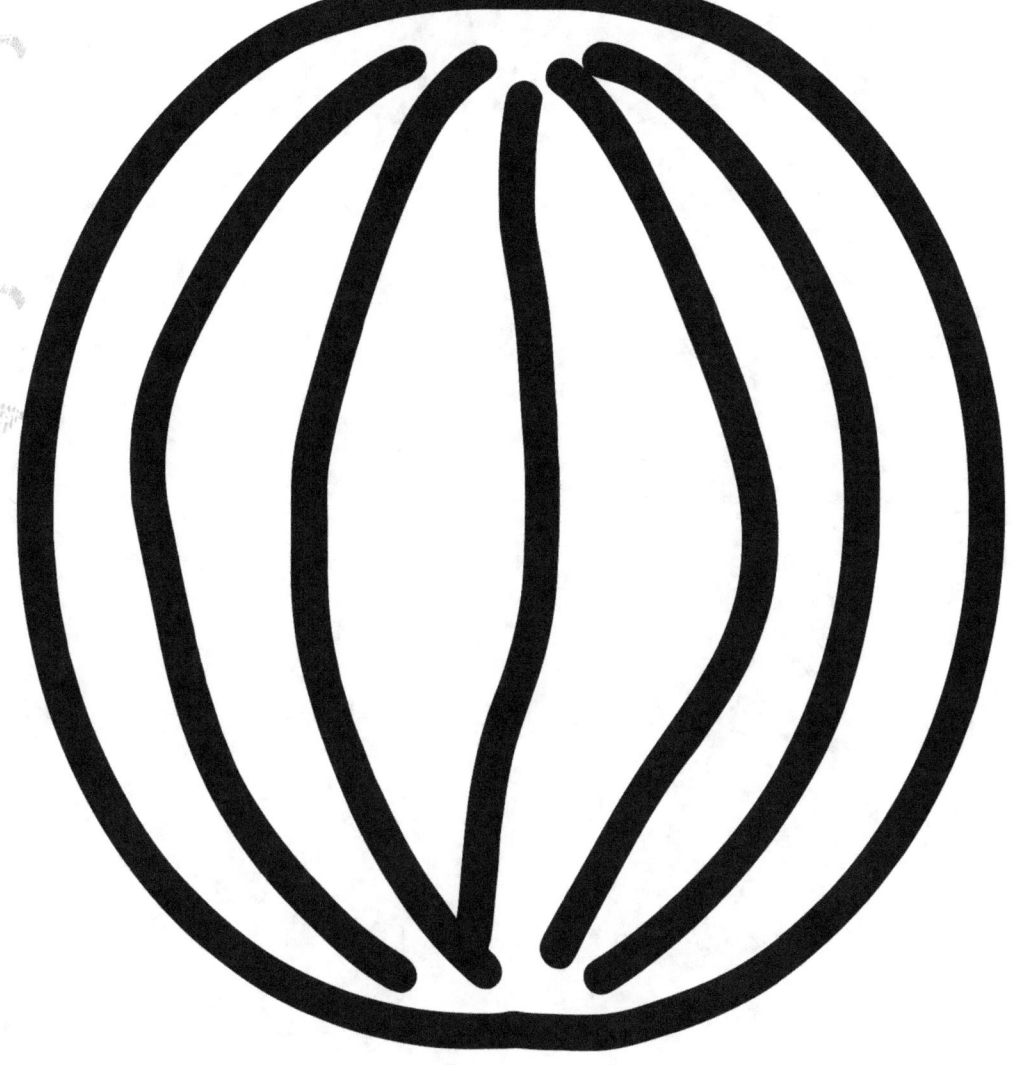

Xigua

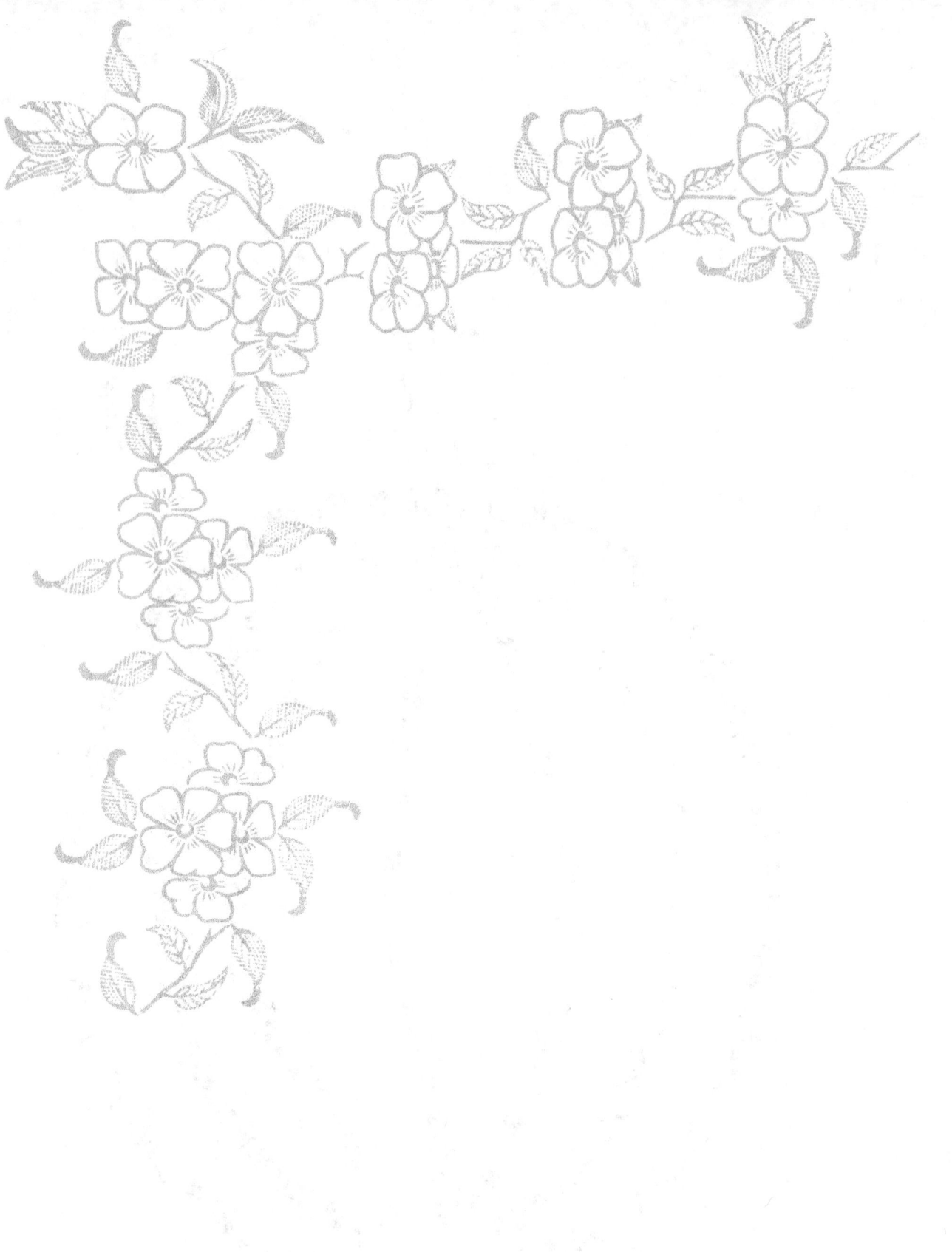

Y for

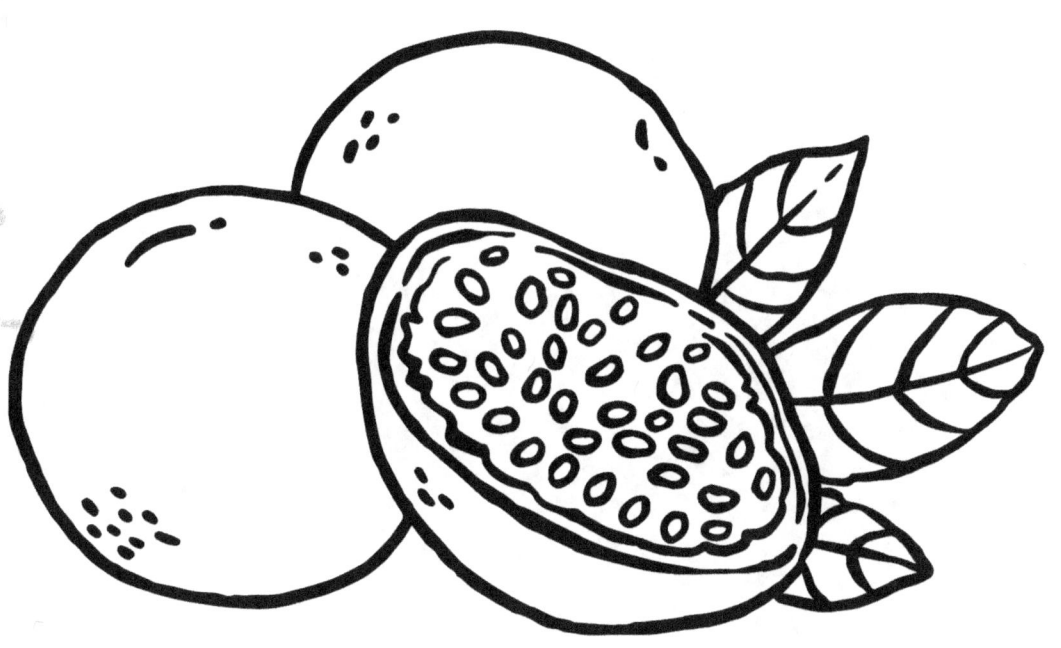

Yellow Passion Fruit

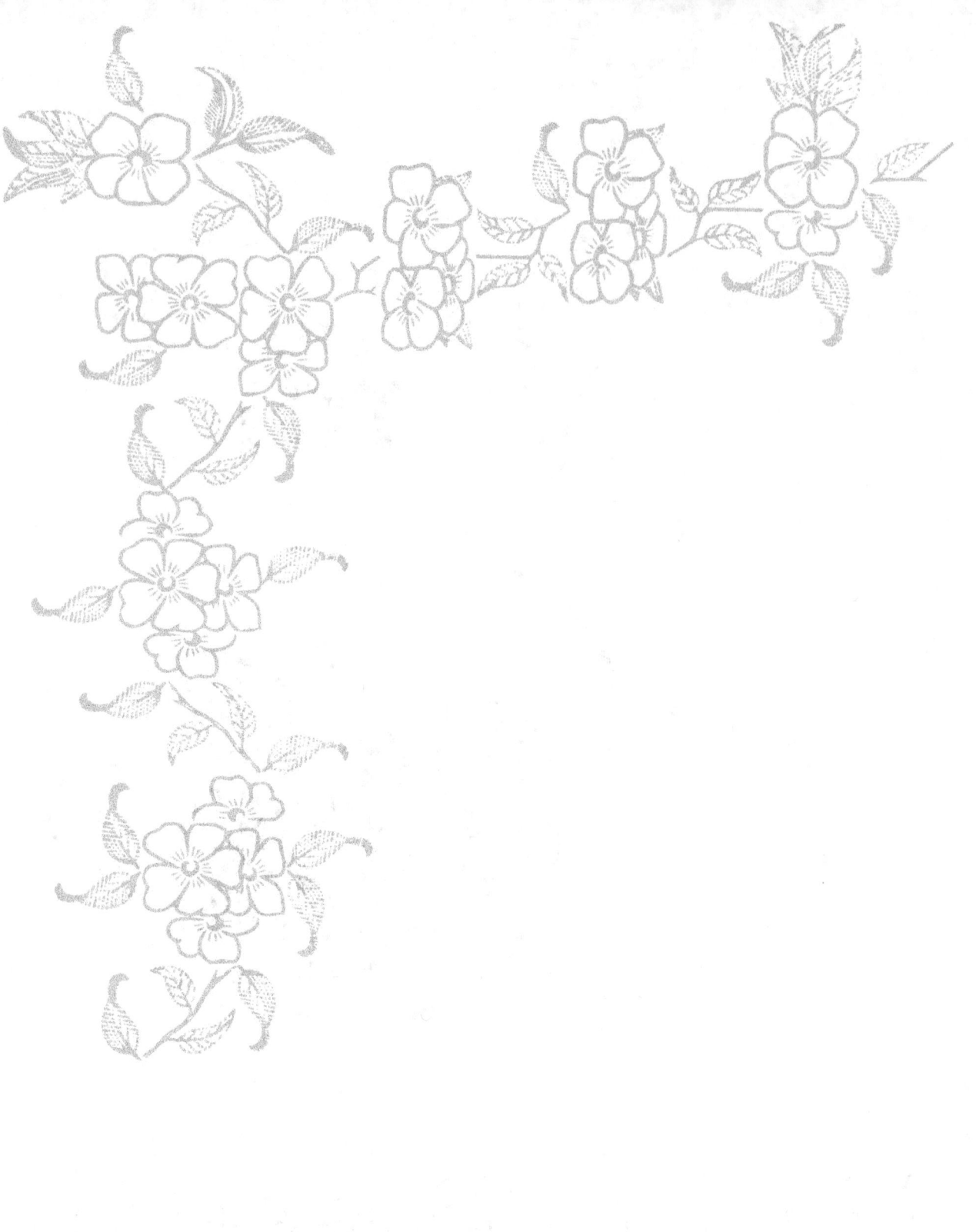

Z for

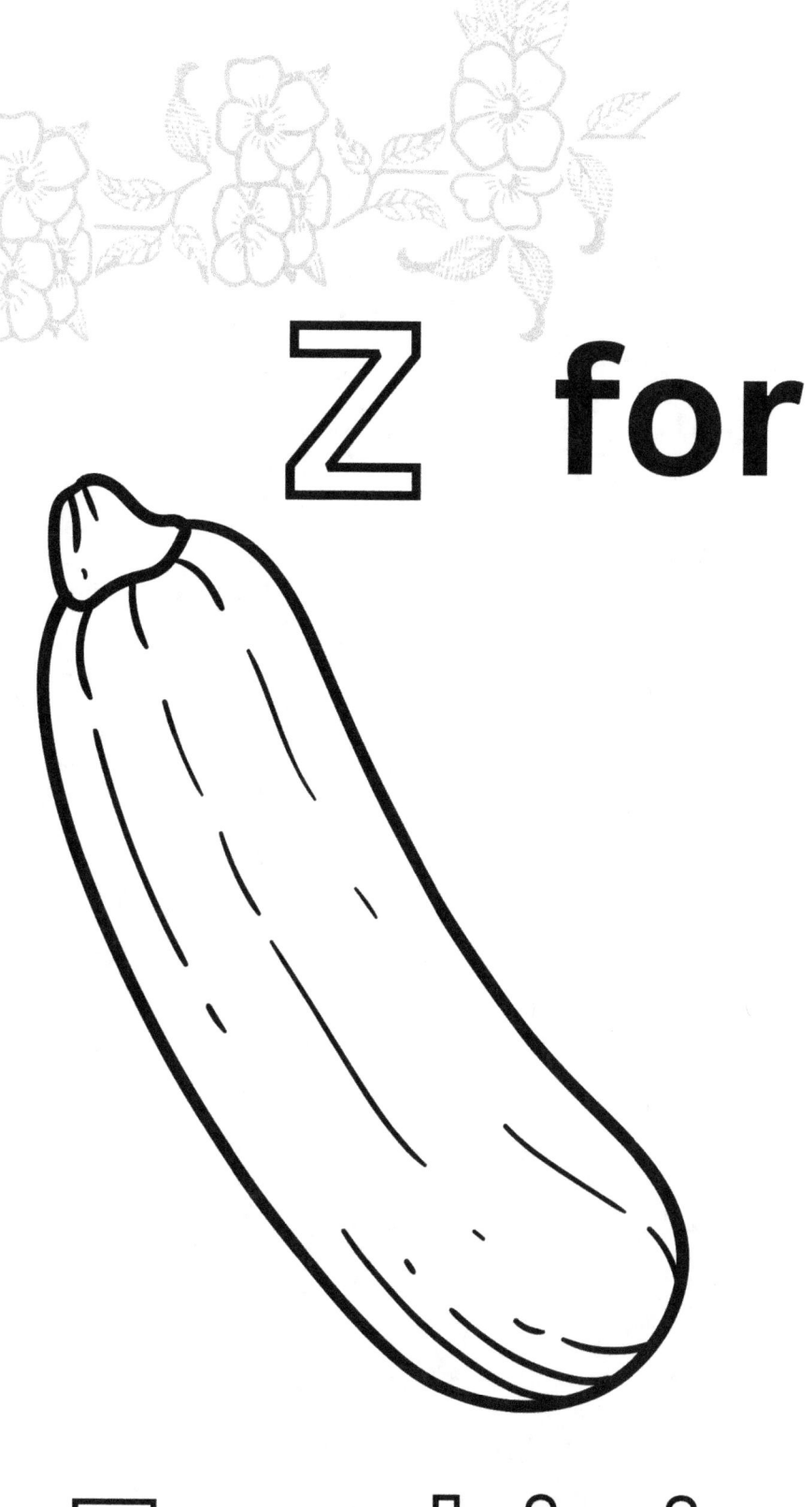

Zucchini

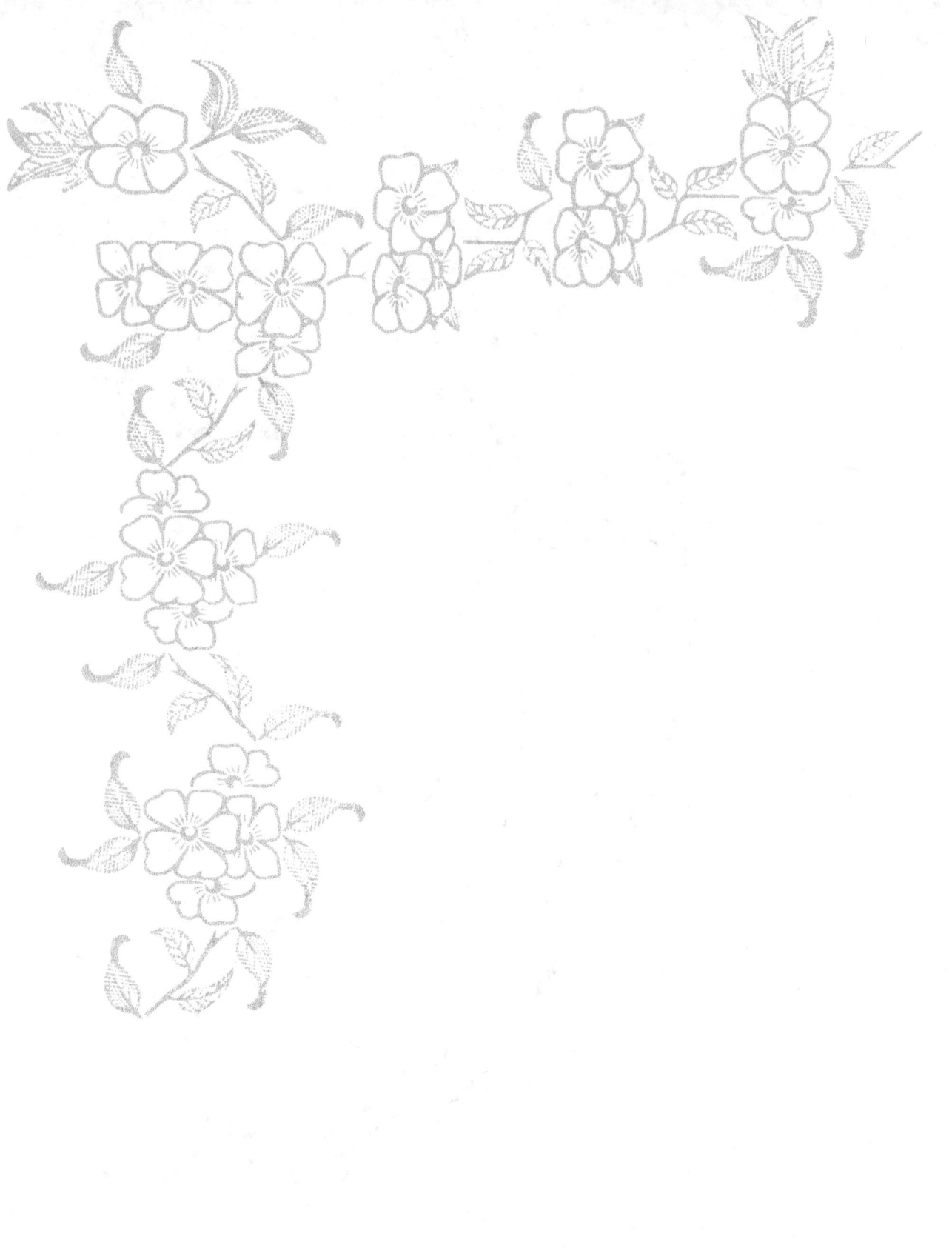

www.ingramcontent.com/pod-product-compliance
Lightning Source LLC
Chambersburg PA
CBHW081019240526
45471CB00017B/3446